12 Ways to Retire on Less

12 Ways to Retire on Less

Planning an Affordable Future

Harriet Edleson

ROWMAN & LITTLEFIELD
Lanham • Boulder • New York • London

Published by Rowman & Littlefield
An imprint of The Rowman & Littlefield Publishing Group, Inc.
4501 Forbes Boulevard, Suite 200, Lanham, Maryland 20706
www.rowman.com

86-90 Paul Street, London EC2A 4NE

British Library Cataloguing in Publication Information Available

Library of Congress Cataloging-in-Publication Data

Names: Edleson, Harriet, author.
Title: 12 ways to retire on less : planning an affordable future / Harriet Edleson.
Other titles: Twelve ways to retire on less
Description: Lanham : Rowman & Littlefield, [2021] | Includes bibliographical references and index. | Summary: "Using checklists, questions, and practical tips, Edleson walks readers through 12 steps to planning and preparing for retirement that work with any budget and focus on the resources at hand. Not every retiree will have an enormous nest egg, but every retiree would like to be comfortable, secure, and happy"—Provided by publisher.
Identifiers: LCCN 2020056819 (print) | LCCN 2020056820 (ebook) | ISBN 9781538114766 (cloth ; alk. paper) | ISBN 9781538193570 (paperback) | ISBN 9781538114759 (ebook)
Subjects: LCSH: Retirees—Finance, Personal. | Retirement—Planning. Classification: LCC HG179 .E349 2021 (print) | LCC HG179 (ebook) | DDC 332.024/014—dc23
LC record available at https://lccn.loc.gov/2020056819
LC ebook record available at https://lccn.loc.gov/2020056820

To Jack and Sonya
My wonderful parents and guiding lights

Contents

~

Acknowledgments

I would like to thank my publisher, Rowman & Littlefield, particularly my editor Suzanne Staszak-Silva, who believed in the project from the outset. She showed me how to turn knowledge, research, reporting, and insight into a book.

In addition, I wish to express gratitude to Jane Bornemeier and Phyllis Messinger, editors at the *New York Times*, and V. Dion Haynes, real estate editor at the *Washington Post*. Special thanks to friend and editor Joyce Gabriel for her time and written comments early in the process of developing the book. In addition, thank you to the Kiplinger Washington Editors.

Throughout my work life, my sources have been invaluable, as have been those who have shared their stories with me.

A note of appreciation to AARP for the time I spent there, and in particular to David C. John, senior strategic policy adviser at the AARP Public Policy Institute and deputy director of the Retirement Security Project at the Brookings Institution.

A personal thank you to Robert Cole, the voice of reason in my life.

CHAPTER ONE

~

Not Your Parents' Retirement

Why Yours Will Be Different

Age 65 used to be the magic number, the year most people retired.

Yet that golden age has changed. Many are working longer. Even though they may want to retire, it's not always possible.

Many face a financial chasm. They don't have enough money to retire. These are not the Golden Years their parents knew. Some are still paying for children's college education, helping elderly parents, paying mortgages, or all three.

In fact, among those ages 55 to 64, just 54 percent have retirement accounts with a median value of $134,000, according to the Federal Reserve Board's Survey of Consumer Finances. Among older baby boomers, ages 65 to 74, less than half (48 percent) had retirement accounts with a median value of $164,000. Fifty-eight percent of those ages 45 to 54 had retirement accounts with a median value of $100,000. Not surprisingly, among those ages 35 to 44, 56 percent had accounts with a median value of just $60,000.[1]

Median means half of the accounts have more and half have less.

How did this happen? How did so many reach their mid-50s, early-to-mid-60s, unprepared for the kind of retirement at least some of their parents had? Read on to find answers and solutions!

The Great Recession hurt many financially. When the stock market plummeted 777.68 points in September of 2008, it sent shock waves through the pocketbooks (and souls) of many at all ages. Those hit the hardest were on the brink of leaving a longtime position, giving up a paycheck, and sliding into a slower gear, whether they called it retirement or not.

1

For them, the stock market crash meant a 40 percent or greater loss of their portfolio, brokerage account, or 401(k) or IRA. For others, it was perhaps the biggest wake-up call, a reminder of what can happen to financial assets. Housing values plunged in many markets throughout the country, leaving some owing more on their property than it was worth.

The term *underwater* became part of public financial parlance. Some lost their homes. In all, people were hurting, though they wouldn't always admit it.

Fortunately, most markets have rebounded. Foreclosure filings were down 19 percent from the third quarter of 2018 to the third quarter of 2019 to the lowest level since the second quarter of 2005, according to ATTOM Data Solutions, a national property database.[2]

More recently, as this book was going to press, the coronavirus pandemic had hit, creating new financial uncertainty for millions.

In the third quarter of 2020, about 28.6 million baby boomers—those born between 1946 and 1964—reported that they were out of the labor force due to retirement.

This is 3.2 million more boomers than the 25.4 million who were retired in the same quarter of 2019. Until this year, the overall number of retired boomers had been growing annually by about 2 million on average since 2011 (the year the oldest Boomer reached age 65), and the largest increase was 2.5 million between the 3rd quarter of 2014 and 2015.[3]

No Pensions

A key difference between the retirement security faced by baby boomers and those who are younger compared to the prior generation is the decrease in the number of defined-benefit pensions. Instead, these traditional pensions have been replaced with defined-contribution pensions or no pension at all. Between 1983 and 2016, workers eligible for a workplace retirement plan who were only offered a defined-contribution plan skyrocketed from 12 percent to 73 percent.[4]

Change was widespread. The trend of staying with the same employer for 30 or 40 years had shifted. Since the 1970s and before, workers have been on the move, with the aim of reaching their career or salary goals by switching employers once or more.[5]

Some baby boomers wanted challenge and better compensation rather than job security. Others wanted adventure—travel to faraway places, self-actualization, and the fulfillment of long-held dreams.

For many, staying with the same employer meant professional stagnation. If they remained in a workplace where too many others competed for the same promotion or where older workers held onto management positions, advancement was blocked. While some chose to stay, others fled to new employers, leaving behind a pension. Those who took the riskier path, gambling on getting ahead, forfeited financial security for a better title, better immediate financial rewards, or something else they deemed "better." If getting vested in a company's retirement plan required staying 10 years, some chose to leave sooner for an opportunity with another company. As a result, they traded financial security for career development and geographic upheaval.

Mortgage Debt

In addition, mortgage debt has slowed the speed to traditional retirement.

Almost 80 percent of the 41 million Americans age 65 and older are considered homeowners, whether or not they are carrying a mortgage balance, according to the Consumer Financial Protection Bureau, the federal agency created in 2011.[6]

The overall home ownership rate has remained the same in the last decade or so for those 65 and older. Yet more people in this group are carrying a mortgage than were 10 years ago. Older owners holding a mortgage increased from 22 percent in 2001 to 30 percent in 2011, according to a May 2014 report from the Consumer Financial Protection Bureau.[7] In past generations, people were often able to pay off their mortgage before they retired.

"There is a definite trend that older Americans are carrying debt into their retirement years," says Stacy Canan, assistant director for the CFPB's Office for Older Americans.[8] The largest part of the debt older Americans hold is associated with their mortgages, though credit card debt and student loan debt exist as well. Chapter 2 discusses credit card debt solutions.

Layoffs and Buyouts

Further complicating the picture, even for those who had saved for retirement, are layoffs and buyouts. Without a hefty paycheck or what one baby boomer called an "obscene salary," they either stopped saving or dug into savings, retirement accounts, or inheritances. Some companies laid off workers in 2009, and layoffs continued in the years immediately thereafter. It wasn't a pretty picture.

Children in College, Aging Parents

Couples with children are aware of the costs of raising and educating children. What may come as more of a surprise is the need to care simultaneously for aging parents and children. Known as the "sandwich" generation, these people are caught between raising their children and taking care of or at least looking out for aging parents.

Even for those who planned, the fallout after 2009 was devastating. They were caring for or assisting aging parents or paying college tuition when their world cratered. Those with recession-proof jobs were on a glide path to retirement. They'd stayed in their same job or with the same employer for 30 to 40 years and toughed out the seemingly interminable years to wake up safe and secure. They are the minority.

Another financial disruption is typically unique to women's lives—when they take off time or work part-time while raising children or caring for aging parents. While this work is undoubtedly important, that gap in employment can have a ripple effect in later years. It can impact a career path, salary, and the amount of Social Security retirement benefits in later years. Yet there are ways to overcome or at least mitigate the effects, which are discussed in chapters 2 and 6.

Low-Interest Environment

Efforts to grow money have been stymied by the low-interest environment. Fear of loss in the stock market propels some retirees and preretirees to leave their money in money market accounts or certificates of deposit. Yet the stock market has seen record highs (and some lower lows). From 2012 until late 2016, the Dow Jones Industrial Average steadily climbed from 12,000 to almost 20,000. Many people who invested did very well in this economy, though only 55 percent of the US population own stock.[9] By December 2020, the Dow had hit 30,000. In early 2021, the Dow climbed even higher.

Longer Lives

In addition to fewer pensions, another trend complicated retirement: actuaries predict current cohorts will live longer lives than their parents, and many will live into their 80s and 90s.

According to data from the Social Security Administration, a man who reaches 65 today can expect to live, on average, until 84.3. A woman who reaches 65 today can expect to live, on average, until 86.6. Approximately one in every four 65-year-olds today will live past 90, and one in 10 past 95.[10]

Essentially, with advances in technology and modern medicine, Americans are not only poised to live longer but healthier lives as well, potentially a better quality of life than their parents had. In a sea of problems, living a healthier life stands out as a path to prosperity, an opportunity to forge a new chapter or more than one.

With longevity inevitably comes a conundrum: *Will I have enough money to last all those years?* The better question to ask is: How will I have enough money in case I live past 95? Read on for answers.

Biggest Fears

Whether it's paying the rent, mortgage, or condo fee by taking on a housemate or it's moving to a less expensive market, today's preretirees are worried about running out of money in retirement.

It's one of the biggest fears among Americans and others throughout the world.[11] This was especially true in the years following the Great Recession of 2008, but it hasn't necessarily abated as the years have ticked by.

The "most common metric" for determining economic preparation for retirement is the income-replacement ratio—that is, the ratio of gross income an individual has after retirement compared to before retirement.[12]

The good news is that there are other ways to determine how well prepared you are for retirement. How an individual or couple spends income is a better measure of well-being than the actual level of income at any point in time, according to research by Michael D. Hurd and Susann Rohwedder.[13]

They point out that consumption—how you spend your money—changes with age.[14] During peak earning years, when income is at or close to its highest point, resources may be allocated differently than once a paycheck is gone. For example, during peak earning years an individual or couple may spend money on family vacations and later on college tuition. Once they give up their paycheck, they rely on a pension, if they have one, Social Security retirement benefits, and retirement and brokerage accounts, if they have them. They may have to change their spending habits to live on different resources. The keys to enjoying retirement are realistic expectations and a careful analysis of your cost of living and the assets you have or are likely to have.

While this may seem obvious to some, something as simple as a budget eludes many.

To clarify these points, consider what actuaries and financial consultants have to say about it: Traditionally there are two ways to calculate the amount you will need for retirement. The first is to assume you will need 75 to 80 percent of your preretirement gross income, and the other is to create a budget.

The first approach assumes your expenses will decrease as you move into retirement, because, for example, you no longer commute to a job and you take fewer clothes to the dry cleaner. The 80 percent rule can get you started. Yet if you take a detailed look at your anticipated expenses during the so-called retirement period of your life and then take a realistic look at your anticipated income, you can avoid, or at least mitigate, the uncertainty of the so-called Golden Years. Whether on a spreadsheet or a yellow legal pad, calculate your expenses and income.

Whether you have saved well or not, there's still time to plan. Ask yourself, "How can I readjust my lifestyle so that I can afford it?" suggests actuary Anna Rappaport.[15]

Working Longer

The reality is that many baby boomers and those who are younger will work longer, and of those, many will prefer to continue working. According to a report by the Transamerica Center for Retirement Studies, seven in 10 boomers say they expect to work past age 65, already are, or don't plan to retire at all.[16]

Much depends on the kind of work they have been doing, the strength of the field they have worked in, and whether they have the skills or can develop the skills required for a different kind of work. Indeed, whether or when they retire also depends on how much meaning they derive from work and whether they need the money.

Generally a person has three options for working in the later years:

- Continue working in the same field, whether cutting back hours or not
- Phase into a different kind of work that uses the skills and talents they already have
- Work part time at a job that is nothing like what they did before, such as working in a pro shop

It may take time to sort out the right path for you. Often, it's best to consider a number of options before making any decision.

Consider Melissa, a 64-year-old retail executive who was living with her retired husband in Davidson, North Carolina, when I spoke with her. She had thought she would work forever. Suddenly, everything changed at the company where she had been for 18 years, and so Melissa decided to retire. Luckily she and her husband had already been planning ahead for the prior three years, trying to figure out what would be her best retirement strategy. Working with a certified public accountant and financial planner, who also is certified as a life counselor by the Kinder Institute of Life Planning, they had discussed different scenarios for the first year of retirement and beyond. "I knew what retirement would look like ahead of making the decision," Melissa says.[17]

She and her husband pooled their resources. Yet without the additional paycheck, they had to take a hard look at their finances—what they were spending each month on their home, utilities, entertainment, and travel. They decided to pay off their mortgage so they would know exactly what their monthly housing expenses would be. Melissa decided to postpone taking her Social Security, delaying it at least until she turned 66 so that she would get a larger check for the remainder of her life.[18] Between ages 62 and 66, your Social Security retirement benefit increases by at least 25 percent to 30 percent. Between 66 and 70, benefits increase by 8 percent per year in addition to *cost-of-living adjustments*. The COLAs, as they are called, vary; the most recent adjustment, for 2021, was 1.3 percent.[19]

For Melissa, leaving her job meant some adjusting to a different life. When we spoke, she was considering building an art studio. Fortunately she had a partner, so they could work out their finances together.[20] Not everyone who leaves or loses a job has a partner to fall back on, especially one with a pension. They have to anticipate what their expenses will be like in the years ahead on their own.

Most agree that the further ahead you plan, the better off you're likely to be. There is good news!

More Options

Today's preretirees are likely to have more work and social options or to think of more alternatives than their parents did.

If you haven't yet left your long-term position, job, or field and plan to in two to three years, this is the time to think about what you'd like your life to be like when you do. Maybe you can't use your parents as role models, but instead you can craft your own idea of how you'd like to live during the next 20 to 30 years.

Sound like a long time? It is. The best way to think about it is in pieces rather than simply "retirement" as one big phase. For those who have been working in the same place or in the same field for the past 15, 20 years, or more and have been saving regularly, it can be hard to visualize not working and spending down assets. If you're not comfortable with that idea, begin thinking about which activities you'll enjoy after you leave your job, if you still have it.

Dreaming

As George Kinder, founder of the Kinder Institute of Life Planning, advises in his book *Life Planning for You: How to Design and Deliver the Life of Your Dreams*, allow yourself to consider any and all of the dreams you have ever had in your life, whether it has been to learn how to play chess or to travel to the east and south coasts of Australia. Even if you think you'll never be able to afford to do these things, write them down. Once you've allowed yourself the luxury of dreaming, you can begin to think about how you will be able to fund those dreams.[21]

If you prefer to stay in your home of many years, for example, you may realize that doing so will keep you from living your dreams because it's a lifestyle that's too expensive. Before you move into the so-called Golden Years, search within yourself to determine what is most important to you.

Is it living near your grown children and grandchildren? Is it exploring new ideas and places? Is it maintaining a sense of community? Is it moving to a warmer climate?

Chances are, you won't be able to get it all, so aim for your top three dreams. If you have a partner—spouse or otherwise—consult him or her. Write down your dreams on paper, and share them with your partner. If you do this early enough, you'll face fewer surprises down the road. With many two-career couples, there is the timing of retirement to consider as well as your individual and joint dreams and goals.

The more you share, the clearer your plans can be.

Certainly you also can pool your resources to achieve your goals.

If you're on your own, you may have more leeway in terms of how you spend your time but, alas, fewer resources. Try to be realistic without giving up what's important to you. Just remember, you can't have it all ways. You may not be able to stay in an expensive house *and* travel the world in style. Even as you dream, think about your priorities. Perhaps you can travel closer to home or save for travel every other year or every five years. Whatever it is you would like to do, planning can help.

Your parents weren't likely to have had as many choices or weren't as aware of them if they did. While you have many options to consider, too many can make it more difficult to decide what you want to do. If you are able to live with uncertainty as you make your decisions, you'll have an easier time segueing into the next phase of your life.

If you think of the first part of retirement as something of a trial period, it can be easier to adjust. Oftentimes, when people first retire by leaving a long-term position, they feel free for the first time in many years. They speak about how they can do what they want, when they want—something many people have never enjoyed. This situation can lead to too much spending without a plan, so beware.

Most people are likely to spend more on travel and entertainment in the first part of retirement and more on health care in the second part of retirement, not unlike their parents did. Yet they may have a broader perspective than their parents (or not, depending on the family from which they came).

Cutting Back

Those who grew up in a time of prosperity may find it difficult to cut back on spending, yet in order to survive and thrive in retirement years budgeting may be an essential part of retirement planning.

For those still working in a full-time position, cutting back may be optional. For those who lost a job or never found another full-time position, careful spending is a must if retirement savings are not substantial. Having discipline and a good plan in place can allow you to postpone taking your Social Security in order to receive a higher benefit. Chapter 6 discusses this.

Certainly there are those who can't wait to stop working, for whatever reason.

If you can, consider how toughing it out for two to four years or more can make a considerable difference.

Age 62 is one of the most popular times to claim Social Security, yet it can be a mistake if you have other resources or if you can keep your spending to a minimum during a limited period of time. For example, if your Social Security benefit would be $1,000 a month at your full retirement age (FRA) of 66 and you decided to claim your Social Security at 62, your monthly check will only be 75 percent of your full benefit amount—or $750.[22]

In short, by waiting to claim your Social Security payments until age 66, you will get a total of 25 percent more each month for the rest of your life than if you'd started at 62—not including any potential COLAs. For those who can wait even longer, until they are 70, the payoff is even greater, at 8 percent more per year.[23]

There are some caveats to delaying Social Security:

- What do you want to do between ages 66 and 70?
- What is your health status?
- What other financial resources do you have?
- Do you have other financial responsibilities?

Consider these factors before you make a decision to claim Social Security. Unless you were born before January 1, 1954, the federal government has eliminated the option to claim your Social Security retirement benefits at your full retirement age or later, and then suspend them immediately while your spouse receives a spousal benefit until he or she reaches 70.[24]

The person who filed and was suspended then accrues delayed retirement credits when they are 70.

Delaying retirement is essentially short-term austerity for longer-term security. While some may find it unpleasant, even a struggle, the very decision to employ discipline in preretirement years can pay off in a larger check from Social Security each month.

Though only 5 percent of Americans wait until they turn 70 to claim Social Security retirement benefits,[25] it can pay to wait.

If you were able to save through the years, you may have a considerable financial cushion going into your Golden Years. If you didn't or weren't able to save and you are still working, start saving now. Either way, if you begin to cut back your spending now, you'll be in a better situation later. Maybe you'll be able to delay claiming Social Security, even for a year.

Questions to Ask Yourself

If you look back on your life so far, what stands out as something you wanted to accomplish but haven't yet?

- Spending more time with family and friends
- Reaching a major professional goal
- Saving more for the years when you may no longer be able to work
- Learning a new skill such as a language, sailing, sewing, racquetball, tennis, ceramics, photography, oil or acrylic painting, or a computer skill such as Photoshop
- Taking your grandchildren on a trip, whether locally or long distance
- Paring down your possessions to suit your current lifestyle

- Joining an interest group whether religious, spiritual, political, athletic, artistic, or culinary
- Renewing participation in activities you have already enjoyed
- Brushing up on language skills you learned in elementary or secondary school or university
- Taking up sports you played in high school or college or earlier in your life
- Honing professional skills

Values and Priorities

1. What is most important to you in retirement?
   a. Feeling financially secure
   b. Living near my grown children and grandchildren
   c. Staying in my home
   d. Enjoying my life

2. What would you most like to do during retirement?
   a. Continue to work part-time
   b. Retool for a different kind of work
   c. Spend time with family and friends
   d. Travel
   e. Explore other leisure activities that I haven't had time to pursue

3. Which considerations are most important to you in retirement?
   a. Cultural activities—musicals, plays, live theater, concerts, museums
   b. Sports—professional sports, such as baseball, basketball, hockey, soccer, swimming, tennis
   c. Social life—book clubs, dining out, game nights, card games, art classes
   d. Religious observance—living near my place of worship
   e. Health care—access to quality medical care
   f. Medical care—access to medical care for chronic health problems

4. What would you be most willing to give up leading up to retirement?
   a. Cable television
   b. Attending movies in theaters
   c. Eating most meals out rather than preparing meals at home
   d. Taking two or more vacations per year

5. Where do you see yourself living in two to five years?
   a. In the home I live in now
   b. In a smaller space in the community I live in now
   c. In a warmer climate
   d. Closer to my grown children and grandchildren

Considering Relocation

1. If you can only choose one, where do you prefer to live?
   a. Near the water—an ocean, lake, or river
   b. Near the mountains
   c. In a city, a suburb, or a rural location
   d. In a house or apartment
   e. With relatives, if necessary

2. If you had to choose, which age groups do you prefer to live near?
   a. Near mostly people my own age
   b. Near people of a range of ages

3. Whom do you prefer to live near?
   a. My grown children
   b. My grandchildren
   c. Other family members
   d. Friends

4. How do you expect to get around in retirement?
   a. Driving my own car
   b. Relying on family members and friends
   c. Using Zipcar or other rental cars when needed
   d. Carpooling
   e. Using public transportation, such as buses, subways, and trains
   f. Using taxis, shuttles, ride-hailing services, and ride shares

Staying in Place

1. Is your mortgage paid off?
2. Is one bedroom and a full bathroom located on the first floor?
3. Can you walk to and from a supermarket, grocery store, and drug store?
4. Is there public transportation to and from your home?
5. Can you afford to use taxis or ride-hailing services?

Covering Basic Expenses

1. If you wait until at least your full retirement age, will your Social Security check cover your basic expenses, including housing, utilities, and groceries?
2. Can you work longer in your current position, if you have one, to postpone claiming your Social Security another year or two?
3. Can you increase your independent work to increase your income?
4. Can you take on a part-time job of any kind to supplement your income?

Cutting Expenses

1. Make a detailed list of all of your monthly expenses, including expenditures such as your cable bill, transportation costs, and dining out. The Vanguard Group has a retirement-expenses worksheet on its website for calculating expense categories ranging from housing to food, transportation, health, insurance, travel, entertainment, and hobbies.[26]
2. If you believe you will have a budget shortfall in retirement, which skills can augment your income or bring in money otherwise?
   a. Professional skills that you can turn into an independent business
   b. Seasonal work that can augment your income
   c. A part-time job based on a hobby—such as fishing or needlepoint—like working in a retail store related to your hobby so you can share your knowledge with the customers; retailers will appreciate your skills
   d. Finding a roommate or housemate, or renting out a room in your house

~

CHAPTER TWO

Evaluating Your Resources

Creating a Budget

Is $1 million a big enough retirement nest egg? You read about it and hear it all the time. If you are 50 or older, now is the time to be realistic. Unless we include the value of our homes, most of us don't have at least $1 million in assets.

In fact, among households ages 55 to 64, approximately 60 percent had retirement accounts with a median value of $134,000, according to the US Federal Reserve Board's 2019 Survey of Consumer Finances—the most recent survey available. That means half of the accounts had more and half had less; 40 percent didn't have a retirement account.

Those who are younger have saved less. For example, 58 percent of those ages 45 to 54 have retirement accounts with a median value of $100,000.[1]

So systematically evaluating your assets and liabilities is essential. If you are within five years of your target retirement date, it's an opportune time to develop a budget for the first year of retirement. Rather than be blindsided when your paycheck disappears, you'll have a plan.[2]

How Long Will You Live?

The first step is to figure out how long you might live. You can do this by taking into account your family history, your current lifestyle, your overall health, and other factors.

In the budgeting process—the expenses and streams of income you an-ticipate in retirement—estimate your longevity using the Social Security Administration's online life-expectancy calculator.[3]

In addition, take into consideration how long each of your parents lived. Then ask yourself these questions:

- What is your diet like?
- How much and how often do you exercise?
- What is your social network like?
- Do you have any chronic or acute illnesses that could shorten your life?
- Do you drink more than moderately?
- Do you smoke?

Nobody knows how long they are going to live, so don't spend too much time analyzing this. The only thing you can do is estimate potential longevity based on your family history and current health.

The Social Security Administration estimates how long men and women who make it to 65 are expected to live. On average, men live to 84.3 years. Woman live to 86.6 years, on average. A quarter of those who are 65 will live past 90, and one in ten beyond 95.[4] You don't know exactly how your life will go! Aim to have a plan in place so you can live well for as long as you do live.

Sources of Income in Retirement

The second step is to evaluate your resources. Think seriously about these. It's important to understand that your expenses may change as you approach the typical retirement age of 65 or 66. Perhaps your retirement age will vary a bit, but it's a fair starting point. Once you analyze your streams of income and monthly costs, you may have to reset your target retirement date or adjust how you spend now to prepare better for a future target date.

In short, you may have to work longer, or you may want to work longer—or both. This might mean staying at your salaried position a year or two or three longer than you'd originally anticipated, or it may mean continuing to operate your business longer or work in your professional practice longer. Or perhaps you may want to cut back to three or four days in your current job at that point or find less demanding part-time work to combine with leisure.

In May 2015 the Transamerica Center for Retirement Studies reported that 82 percent of Americans in their 60s planned to work past 65 years of age or were already doing so. Of those, 18 percent were not planning to retire at all, the report said. Among younger baby boomers—those in their 50s at the time of the report's issue—59 percent planned to work past 65; among those, 15 percent did not plan to retire, the report said.[5] Yet the 2020 pandemic has taken a toll. "One in five US workers (21 percent) indicate their confidence in their ability to retire comfortably has declined in light of the coronavirus pandemic—and only 27 percent are very confident that they will be able to fully retire with a comfortable lifestyle," according to a Transamerica Center report released in December 2020.[6]

The years just before your anticipated retirement are not the time to make impulsive decisions. Instead, take a realistic look at where you stand financially today and where you'd like to be in the years ahead. What kind of a lifestyle do you want to have during your retirement? If you're able to, working longer can be part of your strategy.

Start by listing every source of income you have or will have when you leave a job with a paycheck and benefits or decide to sell or close a business. Once you take any of those steps, you have eliminated what may have been a considerable source of income. Take your time with this decision. Just because you are in the midst of a difficult or annoying span at work doesn't mean it's time to say goodbye to that steady income. Whatever action you take today will have consequences in the years ahead.

Whether you chose to use a yellow legal pad and pencil or a spreadsheet, get your income and savings accounts in order so you have every number you need or a reasonable estimate. Consider any brokerage accounts, old IRA accounts or 401(k) accounts, inheritances, dividends, interest, certificates of deposit, royalties, savings accounts, alimony, pensions, and Social Security retirement benefits.

Though some Americans may have access to various streams of income, by their late 60s approximately half of Americans get most of their money from Social Security, says Virginia P. Reno, former vice president for income security policy at the National Academy of Social Insurance and retired deputy commissioner for Retirement and Disability Policy at the Social Security Administration. After 80 years of age, Reno says, three-quarters of Americans rely on Social Security for most of their income. Even if you have a pension, experts caution that if you decide to retire at 62 you should consider the impact of inflation, because you could live to 85 or longer.[7]

To find a retirement-expense worksheet, look on the websites of most major financial companies. You can fill in the dollar amounts for categories ranging from housing, food, and transportation to health, travel, entertainment, and hobbies.

Your numbers will depend on your most recent spending totals adjusted for how you expect those numbers to vary during the first year or 2 of retirement. For most people, numbers for travel and leisure tend to be higher during the initial years of retirement and in later years higher for health.

After you've itemized all of your assets and expected income, turn to your expenses. Don't rely on guesstimates. If you're figuring your utility costs, look them up on recent bills. For cell phone costs, do the same. For cable and TV costs, look at the bundled fee you're paying today. In short, get a number for every regular monthly cost you have, including any mortgage payment, vehicle payment, home repairs, real estate taxes and homeowners' association fees, and expenditures for travel, dining out, entertainment, and transportation. Remember dry cleaning, gifts, and charitable donations. If you have kept records, check any maintenance costs on your home for the past five to ten years.

With all of this information in mind, turn to your budget. Most people are likely to have less income in retirement than they have during their working years, especially compared to what they made during their peak earning years. With that in mind, create a budget for the first year of retirement, the first year when your paycheck stops rolling into your checking or savings account, or the first year immediately after you close or sell your business. Remember, this is just an estimate but worth tallying. As you evaluate your potential income streams for retirement, be as honest with yourself as possible. No one else, except perhaps your spouse, needs to know every detail of your financial life. If you feel you need a financial expert, make sure to hire a fiduciary—someone who has your best interests in mind rather than just offering suitable financial advice.

Remember, once you give up that paycheck or sell your business, your income will likely drop considerably. If you are able to phase into retirement by cutting back your hours, the shock won't be as great. I spoke with a 72-year-old art curator who had worked for the same employer for more than 30 years. As she reached her mid-60s, rather than retire completely, she had negotiated working four days per week. Easing out of work has afforded her the time to adjust to a new lifestyle and to think about whether to relocate closer to her daughter and grandchildren.

If you plan to phase into retirement, you'll still have part of that regular paycheck. If not, consider these possible streams of income: a defined benefit pension, a defined contribution pension, a 401(k) plan, stock dividends, certificates of deposit, royalties, savings accounts, alimony, Social Security, and a brokerage account with a combination of stocks, mutual funds, and bonds.

Annuities are another potential source of guaranteed income, yet they are not for everyone, and a topic for a future book.

Another asset that many have—often their largest—is their home, especially if the mortgage is paid off or mostly paid off. If you have not yet paid off your mortgage, consider how much you owe and how long it will take to pay it off.

Or would you prefer to sell and downsize to a smaller, less expensive home? Is now a good time to sell? What is the real estate market like where you live? If you live in a heavily taxed area with good schools but you have no children in the system, consider moving to a nearby town with lower taxes.

Analyzing What You Owe

As you approach the age at which you think you might want to give up your paycheck, claim your Social Security, or give up your business or professional practice, the third step in calculating your retirement needs is to analyze your liabilities.

Liabilities include debt of any kind. Ask yourself these questions:

- Do you have a mortgage on one or more properties? This includes your primary residence, rental property, second home, and vacation home.
- Do you have a home-equity line of credit or a home-equity loan?
- Do you have a vehicle payment, even at 0.9 percent?
- Do you have credit card debt?
- Do you have student loan debt?

Likely your largest liability is your mortgage.

Increasingly, older Americans are carrying mortgages. More than 30 percent of homeowners 65 years of age and older are still making monthly mortgage payments, according to a May 2014 report from the Consumer Financial Protection Bureau, up from 22 percent a decade earlier. And among those age 75 and older, the percentage carrying a mortgage nearly tripled during that period, from 8.4 to 21.2 percent.[8]

"Should you pay off your mortgage and reduce your spending?" asks Lauren Zangardi Haynes, CFP, CIMA, owner of Spark Financial Advisors, and member of the National Association of Personal Financial Advisors. "We run the numbers." Depending on your situation, "it can make sense to pay off your mortgage and cut spending."[9]

Can you earn more by investing the money and paying the mortgage interest than by paying off your mortgage? Consult with a financial expert who can help you determine the best strategy. If you are unable to pay off your mortgage, another option is to sell your home and find a less expensive place to live that you can pay for with the proceeds from the sale of your house. A variety of housing options will be discussed in chapters 7, 8, 9, and 10.

Others argue they need a tax deduction against their income. Yet with the new federal tax laws, all mortgage interest isn't necessarily deductible. Consider your total deductions with your accountant or financial expert before making a decision. Paying off a mortgage isn't an option for everyone: It depends on your total financial picture. It's wise to have some liquidity in case of an emergency. Aim to have six to nine months' of liquid savings on hand to cover monthly living expenses.

Paying Off Credit Card and Other Debt

Heading into retirement with few if any debts will free up your money so you can spend it the way you wish rather than using it to pay down debt. For example, if your mortgage payment is $1,500 a month, your credit card minimum payments total $100 a month, and your vehicle payment is $295 a month, you already owe $1,895 every month before you pay for food, electricity, cell phones, cable and television-streaming services, or any travel and entertainment.

Decide whether you want to carry a vehicle loan into retirement or pay it off while you are still working. If you're part of a couple and live in an area with good public transportation, consider whether or not you actually need two vehicles.

Credit card debt, known as unsecured debt, can be the most problematic. It typically carries not only a financial burden but an emotional one—shame, guilt, or anxiety—as well. If you are carrying balances on several credit cards with interest rates as high as 16 percent or more, aim to pay them off before you stop working. Here are ways to pay off debt:

- Identify any automatic payments linked to your credit cards, and determine which can be eliminated. Then either pay off the card in full or make the payments yourself, instead of relying on automation, to remind yourself just how much you owe.
- Delay or reduce large annual expenses such as vacations or holiday spending for one year.
- Telephone credit card companies to ask if they are willing to reduce your interest rates and waive any late-payment fees. This won't be easy, but it's worth a try.

- As you are paying down debt, pay the minimum on each card first, and then apply any extra funds you have that month to the card balance with the highest interest rate. Once a card is paid off, apply that extra amount to the card with the next highest interest rate.
- If you have a card carrying a small balance, pay it off first as a way to boost your morale. Eliminating one card entirely—reaching a definable goal—will spur you on to reach the next milestone. Continue to make at least minimum payments on all your other cards.
- A *tip:* If you have more than one interest rate on different parts of your remaining balance, the minimum payment will be applied to the oldest balance first, even if the interest rate is higher on newer debt. Any additional payments you make may be applied to debt on the same card at a higher interest rate. Ideally, pay off the entire card.
- Put one or more of your credit cards in a one-year debt-repayment program that will reduce the interest on your card: Phone your card's credit customer service department and ask the representative if such a program exists for your card; then ask to be transferred to the department that handles the program. The company may temporarily lower your interest rate during the year, and you will not be able to use your card, a way to ensure you live within your means.

Practicing Retirement

Containing your overall cost of living before you retire will make your transition into retirement easier. If you are more than 10 years and at least five years from your target retirement date, take some steps now to prepare. If you are still in your 50s, avoid increasing your cost of living once your youngest child leaves the nest, suggests economist Alicia Munnell, director of the Center for Retirement Research at Boston College. Most people become more frugal when they have children simply because their expenses are greater. In order to stretch their incomes to cover things like college tuition, they have to economize. "All you have to do is not up your lifestyle from that," Munnell says.[10]

Containing your cost of living will make it easier to pay for your retirement lifestyle. In contrast, if you buy a second home, take a second mortgage on your primary residence, enjoy expensive vacations several times a year, and only shop at retail, you're going to ratchet up your cost of living in the years just before you are likely to retire. Watch out!

Tapping into the equity in your home means, for example, that, if your home is worth $700,000 and you owe $100,000 on the mortgage, you have

$600,000 in home equity. In order to use the equity—cash value—in your home during retirement, you can (1) refinance your home and take cash out, (2) obtain a home-equity line of credit, or (3) obtain a home-equity loan.

If you find that paying off or at least paying down your debt will take a year or two or more, try to work longer to pay it off before you embark on retirement or semiretirement.

Your Largest Asset: Your Home

Unless you have a defined benefit pension with a set amount every month, a large 401(k), or a considerable brokerage account, your home may well be your largest asset. If you are carrying a mortgage, it could be your largest monthly expense in retirement. If you have a significant amount of other assets, you may want to pay off your mortgage, as discussed above. Before you make any decisions, the fourth step in calculating your needs in retirement is to ask yourself where you want to live in retirement.

Here are some questions to ask yourself:

- If you are part of a couple, is one of you going to retire before the other? Are you going to pool your resources?
- Do you anticipate staying in your current home?
- Do you own or rent your apartment?
- What other real estate do you own, if any?
- Are you considering downsizing your four-bedroom house to a townhouse or a condominium? Will it be less expensive?
- Would you entertain the idea of moving to a less expensive part of the country or overseas?
- Will your mortgage be paid off just as you retire?

You can shrink the size of your housing, but moving to a smaller space doesn't always save you money. Be aware that downsizing can be financial upsizing. For example, selling your home and moving into an expensive condominium building with an entertainment room, a health club, concierge services, a pool and sauna, and proximity to restaurants can add costs. If you do make that move, put those costs into your retirement-planning budget.

If you are considering selling your home, before taking any concrete steps, analyze your current and future finances. Be realistic about possible expenses down the line. For instance, if you live in a condo and the building's board hasn't stockpiled a reserve for capital improvements, you may be hit with a one-time assessment or monthly assessments for a year or more. Evaluate how much your current home is worth by obtaining a professional appraisal and decide whether you'd be willing to downsize locally, downsize and relocate, or relocate to a bigger place that would cost less. According to a recent survey conducted by Merrill Lynch and Age Wave, 51 percent of people who have relocated in retirement said their most recent move was to a smaller home.[11]

Expenses in Retirement

During your first year of retirement, some expenses will decrease. Others may increase.

As discussed above, if you decide to pay off your mortgage, your monthly expenses will decrease.

Otherwise, health care costs are likely to be the most significant change in your retirement budget. They tend to increase during the second part of retirement, typically after age 75 or 80.

Some of your cost will depend on whether or not you have an employer-sponsored plan as well.

Other expenses that may change when you retire include the following:

- Transportation to and from the workplace
- Workplace wardrobe
- Dry cleaning for your workplace wardrobe
- Travel
- Dining out
- Costs of taking classes
- Supplies for hobbies
- Home maintenance

Health Care Costs

To some extent, you can control many of the costs outlined above, but you are less likely to be able to control health care costs. So anticipate how health care costs will change when you leave a job, give up a paycheck, or sell a business.

For example, if your employer has been paying the larger percentage of your health insurance premiums during your employment, check to see what it will cover, if anything, once you retire. Will your contribution be larger?

At 65, all Americans become eligible for Medicare. Traditional Medicare consists of three parts: Part A helps cover the cost of hospitalization; Part B helps cover the cost of physician visits; and Part D helps pay for prescription drugs.

Part C, or Medicare Advantage, is a private rather than federal government health plan that typically replaces Parts A and B and sometimes Part D coverage and that typically has low or no monthly premiums. The catch is that Medicare Advantage limits which doctors or specialists you can see. You are typically required to select a primary care doctor from a network. If you see a physician outside the network, such as when you are traveling, you pay more. With Medicare Advantage, you may still have to pay the Part B monthly premium, but your Medicare Advantage plan may cover part of it. Part D for prescription drugs costs on average approximately $33 per month and typically increases slightly each year.[12]

In your 65th year, beginning on the first day of your birth month, your Medicare coverage will become effective. If you sign up in person or online in a timely manner—beginning three months before your birthday month—the Centers for Medicare & Medicaid Services, within the US Department of Health & Human Services, will send you your Medicare health insurance identification card before your 65th birthday.

In addition, Medicare will send you a publication called *Medicare & You*, the official US government Medicare handbook.[13]

It pays to read at least some of it to familiarize yourself with your benefits and how they differ from the benefits offered by your company health plan or the individual plan you previously bought.

Generally, if you are still working, your private insurance pays the initial portion of any upfront medical costs, and then Medicare defrays the remainder. Situations vary, however, so check your terms carefully. Keep the publication as a reference guide.

As of 2021, the standard cost for Part B is $148.50 per month and increases based on your income. Check your copy of *Medicare & You* for details. If you have specific questions about Medicare, call Medicare at 1-800-MEDICARE, or 1-800-633-4227. The information line is available 24 hours a day, seven days a week, including some federal holidays.

Since traditional Medicare covers 80 percent of health care costs, you can purchase a monthly Medigap or supplemental plan to help pay for the remaining 20 percent of health care costs not covered by Medicare. Part D for prescription drugs is a separate monthly cost.

Traditional Medicare allows you see any physician or medical provider that accepts Medicare. Not all physicians do. In 2021, the Part B Medicare deductible is $203 per year.[14]

Compare that to the deductible on your employer-sponsored or individual plan. It could be a lot less.

If you have chronic health problems that require expensive medications, factor those costs into your budget. If you don't have prescription coverage, you can sign up for Medicare Part D.

For those who have not had a health plan provided by an employer and have been paying for an individual health plan, your monthly health care premium cost is likely to decrease when you turn 65 and are eligible to sign up for Medicare. If you receive or are eligible to receive Social Security benefits, you can access Part A at age 65 for no cost.

If you are still working at 65 and beyond and receiving health insurance coverage through an employer, your costs will be different. Whether they are higher or lower depends on whether the health coverage is available to retirees and what percentage of the employer health coverage you would be required to pay.

Devising a Budget

How are you going to pay for your retirement years? There's no simple answer. If you're like many people, you may not have sufficient funds, investments, and a pension to help you through retirement years. Some planned better: They had higher income throughout the years and were able to save more. Or they lived very frugally, saving for the future. Whatever your decisions have been, what's done is done.

Rather than spend too much time figuring out how you got where you are today, consider how you are going to pay for the rest of your life. Analyze the past only if it can help you avoid mistakes today and in the future.

Think about your current overall cost of living: Will you be able to sustain your current lifestyle in retirement? If so, you likely made a good living for most of your work life, saved, invested wisely, planned carefully, lived frugally, had a significant inheritance—or some combination thereof.

Finding the Right Plan for You

Retirement experts note there are two ways to calculate how much money you'll need when you retire. One is to estimate that you will need 70 percent to 80 percent of your preretirement gross income.

Alternately, you can use the monthly budget method.

Since attaining access to 70 percent to 80 percent of your preretirement gross income may not seem possible in retirement, we are going to focus on the budget approach.

A budget is a "spending plan going forward," says Anna Rappaport, chair of the Society of Actuaries Committee on Post-Retirement Needs and Risks.[15]

Even if you are just two to five years from your proposed target retirement date, you still have time to adjust your spending habits and create a lifestyle that can work for you.

If you are in the 55 to 64 age range, whether you have saved well or not, this is the time to plan. Rappaport says to ask yourself, "How can I readjust my lifestyle so that I can afford it?"[16]

If you are in your 60s, you could be planning to fund 20, 30 years or more. "Depending on what you're spending, $1 million isn't necessarily going to get you through life," says Rappaport.[17]

In a low-interest environment, even if you have significant assets, you'll have to rethink your strategy. "You have to modify your approach to retirement," says Mary A. Wallack, AVP, investment officer with Wells Fargo Advisors.[18]

Some of those within five years of retiring are younger, born roughly between 1955 and 1964. They have more time to plan for retirement, especially if they are using age 70 as a target. If you are 55, for example, you technically could work another 15 years.

Those closer to their target retirement date will have to either work longer, rethink their lifestyle in retirement, or be one of those in the top 1 or 2 percent of Americans net worth–wise.

Whatever situation you are in, take time to dream about what you really want to do in retirement. Read on for how to make it possible.

CHAPTER THREE

~

Reframing Your Golden Years as an Adventure

What Do You Really Want to Do?

Satisfaction in retirement varies. A lot depends on your expectations: What did you anticipate retirement would be like, and what is the reality? It also depends on what life has been like before you make the transition into retirement.

If your expectations are unclear, you may find entering an unstructured period of your life unsettling, even disappointing. Often those who have worked intensely for 30 to 40 years look forward to a time when they can do whatever they want, whenever they want. Or they choose to spend more time with their grown children and grandchildren. Others prefer to work at their own pace, no longer commuting to an office each day. Some want to give back in one way or another such as through pro bono work or serving on a board. Overall, the key to the next part of life is attitude. Health plays a big role too. There are many unknowns, so focus on the certainties. Unless you keep working or have significant resources, your options may be limited. Be realistic, and you will be better able to plan and enjoy your life.

Find Your Purpose

To make the most of the years ahead, define your purpose. What will you do? What will make your days meaningful? Enjoyable? The answers are different for everyone.

I spoke about setting expectations for retirement with Bob McDonald, retired chair, president, and CEO of Procter & Gamble and former Secretary of Veterans Affairs. "The most important thing is knowing your purpose," he told me. This means knowing where you are going rather than "meandering through life without direction."[1]

McDonald is one of those fortunate individuals who knew from an early age what he wanted to accomplish. In sixth grade, he applied to West Point, the US military academy, and ultimately matriculated there when he was 18, in 1971, graduating in 1975. He was keenly aware that he wanted to "free people from communism" and believed by filing an early application to West Point he would increase his chances for acceptance to the elite academy.[2]

At age 67, as of this writing, McDonald says that, if anything, he is too busy, even in retirement. He still maintains leadership roles in companies, serving on the board of directors of the Xerox Corporation, the McKinsey Advisory Council, and the Singapore International Advisory Council of the Economic Development Board.

Not everyone will accomplish what McDonald has in retirement, yet each person can find meaning in their own endeavors. It may take some soul searching and self-evaluation to figure out what you like to do, what you have access to, and what your skills and talents are beyond working.

"You don't have to set the world on fire," McDonald says. "Don't allow other people to define your success for you." Helping one other person in a day can represent success, McDonald says.[3]

Consider Where and When to Retire

Research, planning, getting to know your spouse or partner or yourself better, and the willingness to compromise are all part of determining where and when to retire. "It's no one thing," says Reed C. Fraasa, certified financial planner and registered life planner in Wayne, New Jersey, "but time and place are always two big elements. It's rarely a black-and-white single issue."[4]

It can take five to seven years or more to achieve clarity about when it's the best time to retire, if at all, and, if you are considering relocation, where to live.

To start, think about the ideal:

- What would you like to do if money were no object?
- If you are planning your retirement with a spouse or partner, what do they want?
- How much of what each of you wants fits together?
- How much is so different that it might be hard to meld two lives?

Consider where you've been and where you'd like to go before making any major decisions. Take time to reflect before leaving a long-term job or career position, says Robert Stammers, director of investor engagement for CFA Institute, an association of investment professionals.[5]

Think about what your goals are, as they determine everything else.

- Are you planning to travel, stay in one place, or downsize?
- How much is your life in retirement going to cost?
- Do you have adequate resources to live the life you want to live?
- Will you be satisfied if you have to limit your spending in the years ahead because you retired too soon?
- Will working in one way or another be part of your retirement life?

No matter how busy you are in the years leading up to retirement or semi-retirement mode, reserve time to discuss your thoughts and feelings with your spouse or partner. If you are planning on your own, keep a journal or find a trusted friend who knows you well and can serve as a sounding board.

Consider Kathi and Patrick. Married some 50 years, they know what they like: entertaining, gardening, traveling, and spending time with their children and grandchildren. "I don't like being away from my kids too long," says Kathi, a stay-at-home mother. Though her husband, Patrick, was not as certain as she was about having two homes, Kathi knew she wanted to keep the family home and find a second one that would be easy for their grown children to visit with their spouses as well as the grandchildren.[6]

The couple spent 10 years searching for the right place, considering Marco Island, Amelia Island, and Vero Beach in Florida before finding a new community in Bradenton, south of Tampa. They decided on a home a mile from the beach rather than one closer to a golf course. Kathi preferred swimming in Anna Maria Sound to the Atlantic. In addition, living in Bradenton would mean warmer weather than if they bought a home further north. It seemed to be the kind of life they would like. For them, timing was an issue, as Kathi was ready to retire before Patrick was prepared to leave his banking career of 45 years.[7]

Timing retirement was also an issue for Lucy and George of Old Greenwich, Connecticut, and Sarasota, Florida, who had been living together for 20 years. For them, living separately for part of the year was the solution. When Lucy, an author, was 67, she gradually began to live in Sarasota from October to May, more or less. She wanted to be out of the cold, while George was still working as business administrator for a church in Old Greenwich. She describes the move as a "careful and calculated decision" that works for them. "George and I are still making up our lives," she says. Ultimately, they both plan to spend time in both places. For them, living apart has worked, and their marriage can stay intact. For other couples, that may not be an attractive arrangement.[8]

Inventory Your Interests

Knowing what you enjoy may seem obvious, but your interests and passions can be submerged during years of child raising and working. It's useful to keep an ongoing list of your interests and passions. One attorney in his mid-60s admitted that aside from travel he didn't really have any hobbies and preferred to keep working, though he had retired from a senior-level federal job.

By reflecting on your interests during different periods of your life you can identify activities that appeal to you that you haven't had time to pursue. Write them down so you can go back to your list and make revisions. Or you may find different interests to pursue.

The Arc of Life

One way to look at what has been called "retirement" is to consider the arc of life. From birth through the later years, if you retire at 65 or 70, you might enjoy another 25 to 30 years of life. That is a long time to be living without a plan. While you may feel tired or bored of the routine you have, before you make any decisions, look down the road.

- Review your list of activities and interests, and then consider which ones you are likely to be able to continue to do as you get older.
- Factor in your overall health and any chronic conditions you may have.
- Check your eyesight.
- Consider your mobility.
- If you have listed travel as one of your activities, analyze which trips you will be able to take more easily now and which will be easier when you are older.

Pursuing Your Passion

Some people visualize fairly early in their work lives, if not before, what they'd like to be doing in retirement. Others are not as certain. They don't have an overarching goal or picture of what their retirement years will look like. Among those who do, sometimes it's a passion that has been limited by the need to make a living.

For those who have a particular passion they didn't have time to pursue, preparing to retire or work only part-time can be satisfying and meaningful. For those without a passion that bubbles to the surface, working longer can be a reasonable option, a way to postpone retirement indefinitely and increase a nest egg at the same time.

Now in their 60s, Brian and Heather, who married 34 years ago, both knew they would eventually want to retire so they could sail as often as they wished. One of Brian's favorite books is Joshua Slocum's *Sailing Alone Around the World*. At one time, Brian's father was commodore of the Washington Irving Boat Club in Tarrytown, New York, and Brian enjoyed power boating and later sailing.[9]

It was on a 1983 ski trip to Mont-Tremblant in Quebec that the two met and their lives began to change. Brian was living in New Jersey at the time, working as a mechanical engineer. Heather ultimately moved to be with him, and they married the following year. They have always known they would one day want to retire; they just wanted to be sure they would have enough money to sail. It took them until 2016 to realize their dream.[10]

Untapped Dreams

If you have your own retirement dream, you can make plans to pursue it. But even having a retirement dream may put you in the minority. If nothing springs to mind when you think about what you want your retirement to look like, take some time to think about what you really enjoy in life. Give yourself time to think about it, and over the next weeks and months you may come up with a dream of your own. It does not have to be big. Your dream may be to live near your children and help raise the grandchildren. It may be to spend more time volunteering. Or writing. Or traveling. Or a mix of all of those. There is no one right or wrong answer.

Some people simply haven't had the time to pursue their dreams as they've navigated through life, taking care of the tasks at hand; earning just enough money or simply getting by with the money they make from their daily work has been all they could do. They haven't been able to save very much. Others who have put money each month into a 401(k) plan at work may find that it still isn't very much. Yet inside of some people—even most people—may be an untapped dream—potential—that has remained dormant during their working years.

Though it's not the case for everyone, it's worth thinking about what your dreams are if you are in your 50s or 60s. For some people, that is what retirement is for—to do whatever you want, whenever you want.

Brian and Heather, who for a time lived in Gloucester, Massachusetts, on their sailboat *Ark*, had moved inside during the winter months. In 1991, they situated themselves in St. Petersburg, Florida, where Brian continued to work in engineering and engineering management and Heather in human resources management. In 2000, after years of working for corporations, they bought a tool and die business and the building that housed it a year later. They sold the business and the building in 2016. Yet their plans to retire had been in place for many years. "We prepared for it every day, so it wasn't a shock," Heather told me. They used a spreadsheet to map all their expenses and income from property they had bought over the years and when they anticipated selling each building.[11]

According to one lawyer who has retired from the federal government after more than 40 years, "I can do whatever I want, whenever I want." He retired from his federal job at 68 and hasn't looked back. At 71 he enjoys the pension he earned and the freedom he has each day when he awakens. He and his wife, who is younger and still working in a federal job, visit their second home in South Carolina several times a year but plan to keep their home in Bethesda, Maryland.

If you love your work, and some people do, then you may be one of those who wants to continue to work as long as you can either full-time or in some reduced capacity. If you're tired of working, it's worth thinking about what you'd like to do instead. Don't quit your job just yet!

Realizing Your Dream

If you thought you would have retired long ago, it may not be quite so easy to dream about what you'd want your life to look like. Even if you are still working at 60, 65, or 70, retiring may happen sooner than you'd think.

The first step is to visualize the way you'd like your life to be in the years ahead. Forget what you thought you'd be doing, and instead focus on what lures you today and may in the future. Rather than get mired in the day-to-day, turn the page to imagine the next great time of your life.

Life Planning

Life Planning is a tool that preretirees can use to imagine the life they want and begin to put their plans in motion. "Life Planning is a financial movement dedicated to delivering people into lives of greatest vitality, purpose, and meaning," writes George Kinder, coauthor of *Life Planning for You: How to Design and Deliver the Life of Your Dreams.* He founded the Kinder Institute of Life Planning and is a certified financial planner and a registered life planner.[12]

Once they retire, Kinder told me "couples may be spending a lot more time together, and they're anxious, fearful about that." Sometimes, he says, "each has been sacrificing something of themselves to keep the routine going."[13]

So when looking ahead to retirement, each person has the opportunity to think about what they would like to do in this next part of their life, whether as a couple or on their own. "Today you have a much broader range of choice," Kinder says.[14]

Part of the Life Planning approach is explained by the acronym, EVOKE—standing for *exploration, vision, obstacles, knowledge,* and *execution.*

Kinder says that in the first phase, exploration, we have "permission to bring everything in our life, everything we have ever dreamed of, into the conversation."[15]

Ask yourself, if you were not working, how would you like to spend your time?

- Do you want to travel?
- Do you want to live near the ocean?
- Do you want to live in the mountains?
- Do you want to move closer to your grandchildren?
- Do you want to pursue a lifelong interest that you haven't had time for up until now, such as painting, chess, bridge, philanthropy, tennis, or sailing? Is it swimming in the ocean that would make you happy, or perhaps cruising on an oceangoing vessel?
- What kind of life does your spouse or partner have? Or are you on your own?

It's useful to dream about the kind of life you want. Maybe your dream is awaking every day without the help of an alarm or taking off in your convertible at a moment's notice.

Remember, what may be enjoyable, interesting, or exciting for a few months may not afford the same pleasure if it's repetitive.

Before you decide to give your employer notice, consider it carefully. If you are tired of the routine, irritated by the monotony or the commute or the responsibility of answering to someone day in and day out, or any combination thereof, take your time in making major life decisions. While your present circumstances may not always be comfortable, they come with a prize—a paycheck at regular intervals.

If you're approaching 60, quit your job, but then change your mind after a year or two, it's not going to be easy to get back into the workforce. If you're past 50, it's likely to be a challenge as well. Unless you have hundreds of thousands in savings or a defined benefit pension, proceed carefully.

If you are closer to 65 or to 70, the decision to give up your professional life is a bit different. Now that you have made the transition into your 60s, you have the option to access Medicare at 65 and your Social Security benefits at 62 or older.

If you've worked very hard for 35 or 40 years, you may be ready for a different type of life. If you've raised children, paid for college, graduate school, and even professional school for them, and have been able to save as well, it may be time for a big change.

But how much money you have saved isn't the only indicator of whether it's time to give up that paycheck, sell a business, or leave a professional practice. Certain situations can either impede or speed your transition to retirement.

For example, caring for aging parents while you're in your 50s can necessitate leaving your work earlier than you had anticipated. Even if you had expected to one day return to the workforce, it may be more difficult after a gap in employment. Similarly, leaving the workforce to raise children can affect your ability to return to full-time work at the same level when you are ready.

In addition, exiting the workforce for any reason for a period of time ultimately can affect not only the number of years you work but at what income level. This, in turn, impacts not only your preretirement income but your Social Security income whether you claim it at 62, 66, or not until 70, or anytime in between.

Whatever your situation, deliberate and careful planning can help you avoid regret. If you have misgivings about decisions you've made at earlier periods of your life, it may be useful to reflect on how and why you made those decisions, especially if it helps you make better ones in the future. Beyond that, the best approach is to focus on your choices in your current situation.

Retirement as defined by previous generations looked different and, likely, was of shorter duration. For example, baby boomers' parents didn't necessarily expect to live as long as they did or as long as the baby boomer generation and those who are younger are expected to live. That can be 90 years or longer, as discussed in chapter 1.

My father, who lived to 87, enjoyed what one of my first cousins described as a "long and, at times, exciting life." For me, there is a lesson in that—one I often think of as time speeds ahead or slows down, depending upon what I am doing and with whom. Yet I have become philosophical about life, and recognizing that life is filled with peaks and valleys increases joy—at least for me.

A Time of Reckoning

With careful reflection, you may see a path to the retirement you know would be most meaningful to you. This is what George Kinder calls "lighting the torch," a time of reckoning. "It's the moment when we realize the dream we have held onto all our lives is achievable," Kinder writes. Alternatively, it can be a "terrifying moment" when we realize that, "without action on our part, our most precious dreams might slip away."[16] This is when you come to terms with the vision you have for your life in the future.

Once you have allowed yourself to tap into what means the most to you, consider how much that lifestyle will cost. Will you be able to afford it? This is discussed in chapter 4.

Obstacles Other than Money

One obstacle to living the retirement of our dreams, other than money, is internal or relationship conflict. Do you believe that you and your spouse or partner may not want the same things? Part of the value of dreaming is to allow yourself to think about what you want and then share it with your spouse or partner or other loved ones. You may be surprised how similar your dreams are. And you may also be surprised at how different they might be. But there can be room for flexibility and adaptations. The first step in resolving the conflict is to share your dreams, either together or with the help of a certified life planner. You may be able to blend your goals or execute them sequentially. You may do some things on your own or support your partner in pursuing one of their solo ventures. Allowing for a variety of options may help keep both partners happy and engaged.

Finding Reachable Dreams

It's okay to dream, but keep the dreams reachable so you will enjoy this part of your life more. Rather than considering just one way of living these years, experiment mentally and on paper with different scenarios.

Begin by asking yourself some questions:

- If you stay in your current home, what will it cost you?
- If you move to a different home, what will that cost?
- If you move to a different part of the country or world, what would it cost?
- Ask yourself, how important is your current community, and how important is it to be near family members—grown children and grandchildren?
- How important is it to find a lower cost of living so you can travel more or visit family and friends?

Postponing the Dream

If you're waiting two or more years in order to retire with more resources, keep that in mind as you continue to work. Whether you are postponing retiring from a nine-to-five job or from part-time work or selling your business, remind yourself why: You want to get a larger pension or to be vested in a pension at all. You want to get a larger Social Security check at 66 or 70. Or you enjoy your work so much or enough that you want to continue to pursue it as long as you can. This is discussed in chapter 5.

Now that you've considered your dream, read on to analyze how much it will cost and how you can pay for it.

CHAPTER FOUR

~

Funding Your Retirement Dream

Analyzing the Cost

Now that you've analyzed your retirement dreams (chapter 3), it's time to figure out their cost.

If you're within five years of your target date of leaving your full-time job for good, develop a budget or spending plan based on your income after you leave your full-time job or sell your business. It's a good way to avoid being blindsided when you stop bringing home that paycheck.[1]

Housing is the largest single item in most people's budgets, so consider how much you want to spend on it in retirement. You already know your costs in your current situation. If you don't, reread chapter 2 to refresh your memory on how to calculate your current costs and resources.

As you approach retirement, you may want to lower your costs based on anticipated lower income or simply to free yourself from financial burdens you don't need. For example, if you have a second (or third) home, is it an expense you want to carry into retirement?

Projected Lifespan

It's useful to consider longevity before you create a budget—expenses and resources you expect in retirement. If you retire in your 60s, for example, you might live another 20, 25 years or more.

"The arc of life has lengthened," says Andrew Scott, coauthor with Lynda Gratton of *The 100-Year Life: Living and Working in an Age of Longevity* and professor of economics at the London Business School. "We're fitter and healthier for longer. How long are you going to live? You have to think in terms of the future."[2]

For an estimate, use a life-expectancy calculator, such as the one on the Social Security Administration's website. Or start by looking at how long your parents lived (or are living) and your own health. "Most people are going to live longer than their parents," Scott says.[3]

As of this writing, the actuarial table on the Social Security Administration's website estimates that men who are 65 today are expected to live to be a bit older than 84 years of age and women to just over 86.[4] But that is just the average; others will live longer.

Initial Budget

Your budget ought to show all of your current monthly expenses and those expected monthly expenses you will have during the years after you have given up your paycheck or have sold or closed your business or professional practice. Develop an initial budget based on what you expect to spend during the first year of retirement. Be prepared to adjust it as your retirement lifestyle develops over time.[5]

If you feel your retirement resources will fall short of your current or anticipated expenses, "back into a simpler easier lifestyle," advises Joe Ready, head of Trust and Fiduciary Services and chief fiduciary officer in Wealth and Investment Management at Wells Fargo & Co., "especially if you have no dependents at this point in your life."[6]

When preparing your line-item budget, Ready says to ask yourself, "What expenses will I continue to have in retirement, and which will go away? You might find some current expenses will not be there when you retire." For example, if you decide to downsize your four-bedroom house to a townhouse, your housing expenses are likely to be less.[7]

You won't be alone in making changes to simplify your life. As many as 40 percent of retirees do downsize and/or relocate.[8] Chapters 7, 8, 9, and 10 cover various aspects of this topic, from aging in place or not and using your home to fund your retirement to housing options other than your long-term home and choosing your dream location.

For now, focus on your resources.

Assets and Liabilities

When imagining your life in the years ahead, evaluate all of your assets and liabilities. Unless you are among those who already have paid off their mortgage, housing is likely to be your biggest expense and could be among your greatest assets as well. Even if you have paid off your mortgage, there are real estate taxes, condominium or co-op fees, and, sometimes, assessments to pay.

Besides mortgage debt, determine what other debt you have as you are considering retirement:

- vehicle payment
- credit card debt
- other installment loans, such as for a boat

Then list all your other expenses:

- property taxes
- common charges
- periodic home repairs
- utilities
- groceries
- dry cleaning
- shoe repair
- cable
- landline
- cell phone
- health-insurance premiums
- vehicle insurance
- homeowner's insurance
- dining out
- other entertainment
- transportation
- travel

What are your streams of income?

- pensions
- Social Security
- dividends
- 401(k)
- rental property
- income from part-time or other work

Typically, major financial companies offer retirement-expense worksheets that can help you pencil out your budget. For example, the Vanguard Group has a worksheet to help you tally your monthly anticipated retirement expenses that lets you put in dollar amounts for categories ranging from housing and transportation to food, health, travel, entertainment, and hobbies.[9]

First Year versus Later Years

Your numbers will be based on what you have been spending in each category and how you anticipate those figures to change during the first year or two of retirement. Often people spend more on travel and leisure pursuits during their initial retirement years and more on health care in later years.[10]

Each person's situation is different, so consider your projected expenses as you move into retirement. Will your retirement income be able to support the lifestyle you envision? If not, evaluate your priorities and how you may be able to trim your expenses in specific areas.[11] Will you limit your cable package in favor of dining out more often? Can you check out books from the library rather than purchasing every book you wish to read?

Budget in Flux

A budget is not a one-time event but a yearly exercise to see where you've been in the past year and where you're headed. This can be the tricky part. You have to be honest with yourself and, if you have one, your spouse or partner. As you prepare your detailed spending plan, ask yourself which expenses will continue as they are, which are likely to decrease, and which will likely increase. For example, for something as simple as your cell phone, cable bill, and house phone, is the cost immediately going to increase upon retirement, or can you eliminate some of your costs by getting rid of the bundle and keeping just your cell phone? If you use ride-hailing services instead of public transportation, include those costs. This is where priorities come into play.

List every current and anticipated monthly expense you will have during the years when you may have less income than today. From there, create your initial budget for retirement based on what you expect to spend during the first year of retirement. Once you have that as your base, be prepared to adjust it as your retirement lifestyle develops in the years ahead.

Reaching Your Goals

Finally, reflect on what you'd like the Golden Years to look like, and consider how to reach those goals. Review chapter 3 for ways to think about these years.

- Are you going to downsize, relocate, live on a houseboat?
- Do you have grown children and grandchildren to consider, or is it just you—or you and your partner?
- Do you want to move to live near family members, even though they may decide to move for work or for other reasons?
- Do you want to stay in your current location but find a less expensive place to live that requires less household work?

Several Retirement Scenarios

Imagine different ways you might retire to narrow down what is most important to you. Rather than consider just one way of living these years, experiment mentally and on paper with different scenarios.

For example, what would it cost if you were to . . .

- stay in your current home?
- relocate to a different home?
- move to a different part of the country or world?
- choose to live in an active-adult or other planned community?

How important is it for you to . . .

- stay in your current community?
- be near family members—grown children and grandchildren?
- find a lower cost of living so you can travel more or visit friends and family more often?

Years before they retire, some people begin to plan. As the years go by, some decide they are going to work until they are 70. For example, one couple who moved from the Washington, D.C., area to San Antonio in 2019, had decided that they would both wait until 70 to claim Social Security benefits. (They were actually eligible to use the file-and-suspend strategy that was eliminated with the Bipartisan Budget Act of 2015; he claimed at 66, then immediately suspended his benefits, and she was able to receive spousal benefits until she would claim her own, higher, amount at 70.)

The couple had lived in several cities during their marriage and while raising children and considered where they might want to live in retirement.

Though they liked Gainesville, Florida, they decided to return to San Antonio in 2019, where they had previously lived for 10 years. They like the city, and their older daughter, who is married with two children, lives there. Their younger daughter, who is married with one child, has since moved there as well.

The cost of living in San Antonio is lower and the weather warmer than in the Washington, D.C., area, where they also had lived for 10 years. One of the appeals of Gainesville had been that it is a university town in a mild climate.

Whether you've thought about retirement from the time you began working or your target date is five or ten years away, figuring how you will pay for your dreams will help ease uncertainty. Having a written plan will make the financial transition to retirement smoother.

In addition, if you find your dreams exceed your resources, consider working longer, as discussed in chapter 5.

CHAPTER FIVE

~

Working as Long as You Can

If you thought by the time you were 65 you'd be lying on a beach in the French Riviera or any beach, or riding a golf cart on an Arizona course, you may be in for a surprise. Be prepared for something different.

You already may have realized that traditional retirement isn't for you for any number of reasons. You like your work too much; you like your work more than most other activities; or you need the money. It could be a combination.

Whatever the motivation, like others, you've chosen to keep working in one way or another.

When you look ahead, you're realistic. At 65, you could well live to 90 or 95. Twenty-five or 30 years is a long time.

In fact, research shows that baby boomers anticipate working past 65 or already are. Seven in 10 boomers say they either expect to work past 65, already are working past 65, or don't plan to retire at all, according to a Transamerica Center for Retirement Studies report. "Baby Boomers (born 1946 to 1964) have rewritten societal rules at every stage of their life—and retirement is no different," the report says. "They are at the forefront of defining retirement as a new phase of life that can bring freedom, purpose, and enjoyment."[1]

Financial considerations drive 80 percent of workers planning to work past 65 while healthy-aging reasons drive 72 percent. Furthermore, though many baby boomers expect to work beyond 65, few are preparing themselves

by focusing on their health, keeping job skills current, and planning financially for a long retirement.[2]

There are a variety of ways to think about work.

First, let's talk about the financial aspect. If you enjoy your work, as many
do, staying with it provides a way to stay active mentally, physically, and
socially. At the same time, the paycheck or checks continue. This is a good
reason to work. If you believe your streams of income won't be enough or will
leave you with too limited a lifestyle if you stop working, it's another reason
to stick with your job

Purpose

Another key reason people work in the years that many people used to be retired is for "the meaning and purpose quotient," says John Tarnoff, author of
Baby Boomer Reinvention: How to Create Your Dream Career Over 50. "They
are used to working with people."[3]

Yet for many in their 50s and 60s, working is a necessity, like it or not.

Whether they were downsized, bought out, or "let go," they find themselves looking for work.

The ideal time to prepare for this potential situation is while you still have
the full-time work and don't yet need to "reinvent" yourself, says Tarnoff, a
former Hollywood entertainment executive turned reinvention coach. "A
side gig" is a great way to segue from full-time work to an entrepreneurial
pursuit that becomes a second career. Essentially, though having a full-time
position in your late 50s or 60s may seem like security, it can backfire not
only in terms of money but in a sense of purpose as well. "The security is an
illusion," Tarnoff says. "It's a trap."[4]

How do those in their 50s and 60s who are suddenly out of work survive at
first? The fortunate ones have paid off the mortgage on their home, have just
enough to get by with consulting work, have considerable savings, or have
spouses or partners working full-time.

Searching

When looking for that next source of fulfillment and income, the challenge becomes moving beyond the precise kind of work you have done and
reframing your work history and yourself. When Tarnoff first meets some of
these baby boomers, "they're in a complete freeze moment." They're scared:
"I don't know how I am going to earn a living for another 20 to 30 years,"
they tell him.[5]

He estimates that 85 percent of jobs are filled through referrals or in-house employees, so e-mailing résumés typically isn't going to be an effective way to find a new position. You have to consider the value that you are offering, Tarnoff says. After working for 30 or 40 years, most people know what their skills are and what they like to do. "They have to leverage what they have in ways they haven't thought of," he says.[6]

Rather than just revising a résumé, which can be helpful, older workers have to assess the skills they have as well as those they are lacking that might be valuable in today's labor market.

Paths to working for older Americans vary. Consulting, seeking specialized knowledge and new contacts from working as a volunteer, enrolling in online courses or at a community college, or starting a business are all options.

Updating Your Skills

"If you have been laid off or retired for a couple of years, skill sets may have moved on quite rapidly without you," says Mark Schmit, executive director of the SHRM Foundation, a research affiliate of the Society for Human Resource Management. "This puts you at a disadvantage to the people who are working, including peers who are the same age."[7]

To return to work, a key credential is documenting your technology skills, according to Rich Feller, a professor in Colorado State University's Counseling and Career Development program and past president of the National Career Development Association. If you can do this, employers will "overlook your age," he says. He recommends taking community college online courses to develop new skills.[8] In addition to updating your skills, building your network of contacts is important. "If you know someone who can provide an entrée, anyone who can tell you more about the company, if nothing else, pick their brain—what is the best way to approach that company?" says Rick, who began taking courses at Montgomery College, just outside of Washington, D.C., at 58 while looking for his next job in Web development. He had worked in sales for 30 years."[9]

If you have been retrained for a different career, it might mean starting at a lower salary. "It takes a certain amount of courage," says Dave, who at 61, after 30 years of working as an employee, took a five-week class to prepare for the real estate broker's exam in Colorado. After passing, he joined a regional real estate firm.

Even though he had worked in sales in the past, he found the best approach to his new work was to learn new techniques and "be pliable."[10]

Impact on Social Security Benefits

Okay, so you've found some work. Be aware that if you haven't reached your full retirement age—66 for those born between 1943 and 1954—and already have claimed your Social Security retirement benefits, you will be faced with the earnings test. This means you can only earn up to a certain amount of money before the Social Security Administration (SSA) will withhold some of your benefits. The earnings limit varies by year. For example, for 2021 that limit is $18,960. If you are younger than your full retirement age, SSA will withhold $1 for every $2 you earn above the limit.

During the year you reach your full retirement age, SSA will withhold $1 for every $3 you earn above the limit. For 2021, that earnings limit is $50,520. Once you reach the month of your full retirement age, you can earn as much as you wish, and no dollars will be withheld.[11]

The good news is that if your earnings during those years are higher than previous years, SSA will recalculate your future benefits each year by substituting the higher earning years for previous lower earning years.

SSA uses the income from your highest-earning 35 years to calculate your retirement benefits. For example, if you went back to work at age 65 and earned a higher salary than you had in previous years, that year would become one of the highest earning years used in the SSA calculation. So in the long run, working longer has several benefits:

- You'll have the earnings while you are working.
- You can save or invest those earnings.
- If you are working at a higher salary, your earnings may increase your future Social Security benefits.

Just remember, if you find a job while you are collecting Social Security retirement benefits, be sure you contact the SSA to let them know. Otherwise, you may receive more benefits than you are entitled to and be required to pay back the overpayment.

Indeed, more people past 60 are working than not. More than half—54.7 percent—of Americans ages 60 to 64 were working at least part time in 2017, according to the Bureau of Labor Statistics. Among those 65 to 69, almost a third were working.[12]

For example, Ron postponed retirement until 68 and opted to take his Social Security retirement benefits at 65. "I was waiting until my wife got closer to being able to draw Medicare," he says. He retired as a partner in an insurance agency in Fort Worth, Texas, sold his stock in the agency, received a down payment, and was to receive monthly payments for 6 years thereafter. His wife was 64 at the time. For Ron, who had been saving since he was in his 30s, spending money to travel with his wife while continuing to save were priorities.[13]

Bridging Shortfalls

Though everyone doesn't anticipate a lump-sum payment and subsequent payments as retirement approaches, they find a way to survive—even thrive. "People are very practical and will find a way to earn money to bridge savings shortfalls," says Catherine Collinson, president of the Transamerica Center for Retirement Studies.[14]

Indeed, staying at your full-time job or running your business or professional practice as long as you can is one way to keep engaged while money continues to flow. But sometimes that period of your life ends unexpectedly, or you decide to move on.

Be Prepared

If you think your full-time work may come to an end for any reason or no particular reason, prepare for the time when you might find yourself without a paycheck or income from a business or professional practice. People may intend to work indefinitely, but health, downsizing, layoffs, age discrimination, and other situations may change your plans. Be ready.

While you are still working, build up rainy-day and emergency funds that can help you through the transition to other sources of income or traditional retirement. Many financial experts say to have four to six months' worth of savings in case hard times hit. Stock market unpredictability is another reason to have easily accessible funds so you won't have to sell stocks, mutual funds, or bonds to get through until you can claim your Social Security retirement benefits. Remember, for those born between 1943 and 1954, the earliest you can claim Social Security is at 62, but that will mean you will receive monthly benefits that are 25 percent lower than if you wait until you are 66. If you were born in 1960 or after, your full retirement age is 67. If you wait until you turn 70, your monthly benefit will increase by 8 percent per year between your full retirement age and 70. Many people aren't aware of this, and only about 5 percent of Americans wait until 70 to claim their retirement benefits.[15]

Aim to have as much as nine months' of expenses in a high-yield money-market account that you can access easily.[16] Some brokerages offer high-yield money-market accounts, but you have to sell your shares first and then move the money into your checking account. If you want to be able to access your money almost instantly, keep some in a high-yield savings account linked to your checking account.

If you are unexpectedly not bringing in any money, a cushion can make a huge difference. In times of stock market volatility, if you have one to two years of expenses in cash, you can avoid beginning to spend down your retirement assets if their market value has declined.

Illness or injury can affect anyone's ability to work at any time, which can mean loss of income. An ear, nose, and throat surgeon in his mid-60s had to curtail the surgical part of his practice due to limited vision, while a maxillofacial surgeon in her 50s felt compelled to sell her practice when neuralgia and subsequent injury left her unable to work. Cash can ease these situations. While the ENT physician, now 71, continues to work, his income has declined.

Financial shocks leading up to retirement can be financially as well as emotionally painful. Unexpected expenses crop up more frequently than people would like to think, according to Brigitte Madrian, dean of the Brigham Young University Marriott School of Business.[17]

Building Savings

To be prepared, have two funds—a rainy-day fund for smaller expenses and an emergency fund for larger ones. Research shows having more than one account helps.[18] Saving isn't necessarily easy, especially if you have been living paycheck to paycheck or month to month on your current earnings.

Typically a rainy-day fund is smaller, up to $2,500—compared to an emergency fund, which can stash as much as nine months of living expenses—$10,000 to $50,000 or more depending on your expenses.[19]

Whichever way you build your cushion, be sure you do it. There is no substitute for the peace of mind that comes from knowing you have funds to cover expenses when you need them. Even if you can only save a little from every paycheck, do it; it's important to have a cushion.

Finding Meaning

If it's not money you need from working in your later years but meaning, there are ways to achieve this. If you're still working and haven't yet given this much thought, begin thinking about it now. What are ways you could continue to work?

- independently
- part-time
- as a consultant
- as a volunteer or in a pro bono capacity, donating your time and/or services
- serving on a board of a nonprofit organization

If you want to work for pay but not in as structured a way or for as many hours as you have previously, there are a variety of options. Among them are phased retirement, a "bridge job" on the way to full retirement, part-time work, a hobby-turned-business, or other entrepreneurial work. Many Americans are working longer, but even more would opt to if jobs were flexible.[20]

Bridge Jobs

The key to finding a "bridge job" is actively seeking one. A bridge job is a temporary position between your full-time career and retirement or that serves as a transition into a new kind of work.

"Among those who directly transitioned to complete retirement after their career jobs," reports the National Bureau of Economic Research, "only 11 percent (147 out of 1,336) report having looked for a new job opportunity. In contrast, 80 percent (657 out of 812) of those who had a bridge job actively looked for such an opportunity, while only 20 percent of workers found their bridge job without reporting searching."[21]

Phased Retirement

A relatively new concept to Americans approaching traditional retirement age is entering a phased retirement. The US Office of Personnel Management (OPM) describes it as a human resource tool that "allows full-time employees to work part-time schedules while beginning to draw retirement benefits."[22]

The advantages of phased retirement for the employee are clear: Rather than retire cold turkey, the worker is able to get a taste of retirement. For managers, phased retirement can "provide unique opportunities for employees while increasing access to the decades of institutional knowledge and experience that retirees can provide."[23] Federal regulations have meant that federal agencies have been able to send phased retirement applications to OPM as of November 6, 2014.

Whatever the other benefits to the workforce, phased retirement allows older workers to gradually explore what it's like to be retired. They can decide how well it works for them. During this period, they can also explore other work opportunities. Older, experienced workers bring "institutional memory" to the workforce as well as the ability to mentor younger, less-experienced workers.

If you want to keep working after you leave your long-time career, it's best to plan how while you still have your career job. For example, one route is taking on consulting work in your field that can lead to more consulting once you've left your career position.

In fact, the gap between those planning to work in retirement and those who actually are has narrowed, with more older Americans continuing employment.[24] Among other options for maintaining a working life in later years is to start your own business, transition to freelance work that you began while working full-time, or turn a hobby into paid work: work in a pro shop at a golf course, in a crafts store, at a sports arena, or in a performance venue.

Meanwhile, figure out the best time for you to claim your Social Security retirement benefits as discussed next in chapter 6.

CHAPTER SIX

~

When to Claim Social Security

Maximizing Your Monthly Check

Deciding when to claim your Social Security benefits can be one of the most important decisions you'll make in advance of leaving your job or selling your business.

The amount of your monthly Social Security retirement benefit depends on how many years you've already worked, how much longer you might continue to work, and at what salary. It also depends on the age at which you begin claiming benefits. If you're armed with information, you can make a better decision about when is the best time for you to claim.

You qualify for retirement benefits based on having worked and paid Social Security taxes, earning "credits" toward future benefits. Most Americans need 40 credits or 10 years of work to qualify for benefits. Even if you have not earned enough credits, the ones you have earned stay on your record. If you return to work after a gap in paid employment, you'll earn more credits. You earn credit by working and paying Social Security taxes. In 2021, for each $1,470 you have earned, you receive one credit. The maximum number of credits you can earn in a year is four.[1]

Creating an Online Account

The first step in managing your Social Security benefits is to go to online to https://www.ssa.gov and create an account, if you haven't done so already, to access your earnings record.

Waiting to Claim

Many retirees know that waiting to claim Social Security benefits can lead to higher monthly payments, yet few realize how much more they can receive if they delay onset of payout, according to Social Security experts. "Many people don't understand how important Social Security will be as a part of their income, especially in later years," says Anna Rappaport, chair of the Society of Actuaries Committee on Post-Retirement Needs and Risks.[2]

If you postpone claiming your Social Security, you can maximize the amount of income you can receive every month for the rest of your life. At age 62, you are eligible to begin receiving reduced benefits. At your full retirement age (FRA)—which is 66 or 67, depending on the year you were born—you are eligible to receive full benefits, typically 25 percent more than if you had begun receiving benefits at 62. If you wait to claim benefits after reaching your FRA, you receive delayed retirement credits, which amount to 8 percent per year between the ages of 66 and 70 or between 67 and 70—again, depending on the year you were born.

In addition to presenting your earnings record online, if you are not yet receiving benefits, your account typically tells you how much Social Security you will receive each month whether you claim at 62, 66, or 70. Of course, you can claim any month or year in between.

Full Retirement Age

For those born between 1943 and 1954, full retirement age is 66. If you were born after 1954, your full retirement age increases to between age 66 and 67.

- If you were born in 1955, your FRA is 66 and 2 months.
- If you were born in 1956, your FRA is 66 and 4 months.
- If you were born in 1957, your FRA is 66 and 6 months.
- If you were born in 1958, your FRA is 66 and 8 months.
- If you were born in 1959, your FRA is 66 and 10 months.
- If you were born in 1960 or later, your FRA is 67.[3]

The SSA calculates how much Social Security you will receive each month based on your 35 highest years of earnings. First, make sure the earnings record is accurate; then consider, based on your total financial picture, when is the most propitious time to claim your benefits. The account will show you how much you earned each year since you began working. Say you had a summer job for which you earned $800 back in 1970; you are likely to see that listed along with the regular full-time jobs you've had ever since.

If you believe you've found errors, you can bring them to the SSA's attention. You'll have to document any income from previous years.

Claiming Early

Though fear has propelled many people to claim their retirement benefits as soon as they turn 62, the earliest possible time they are eligible, it is not always the best time to claim. In short, if you are still working or have other available resources, it's generally best to wait until later. However, the biggest concern many people have is that the Social Security system will run out of money.

According to the Social Security Administration's website, there are two Social Security trust funds—Old-Age and Survivors Insurance (OASI) and Disability Insurance (DI). Until 2035, the two trust funds will be able to pay all benefits in full and on time.[4]

Though the system will not be depleted, the latest projections show that the Social Security Trust Fund can continue to pay out full benefits until 2032. This means that if the US Congress doesn't take action, recipients might receive only 79 percent of their benefits in 2032.

In addition, experts say Congress is likely to adjust the way Social Security benefits are funded, as it has in the past, before benefits would have to be cut in the future.[5]

The Social Security trust funds have "reached the brink of depletion of asset reserves in the past. However, in 1977 and 1983, Congress made substantial changes to the program that resulted in the $2.85 trillion that exists today."[6]

Looking at the Total Picture

The decision regarding when to claim Social Security retirement benefits is a highly personal one; it must be made on a case-by-case basis. Before tapping Social Security, consider your entire situation:

- Are you still working?
- Do you have any chronic medical conditions that could shorten your life?
- How long are you likely to be able to keep working at the salary you have?

- What other financial resources do you have that you can use as a way to postpone taking Social Security?
- What is your life expectancy? For this, consider your current health: Do you have any chronic health problems? How long did your parents live? How fit are you? What kind of lifestyle do you live?

Indeed, experts remind Americans how much is at stake if they claim early. Unless you are unable to pay your rent, for example, or have a chronic health problem that is likely to shorten your life, it's best to wait.[7]

Working to your full retirement age—66 for those born between 1943 and 1954—gives you approximately 25 percent more in Social Security benefits than if you were to begin taking it at 62. If you wait until you've turned 70, you can expect to receive 32 percent more between ages 66 and 70 or 8 percent more per year.

For every month and year up to age 70 that you delay taking your Social Security benefits you will receive a larger check for the rest of your life. However, if your full lifetime ends up matching the national average, Social Security says that you will get the same amount of money over the course of your life. You either get more, smaller checks or fewer, larger checks. For those who believe they might live beyond the average lifespan, waiting until 70 can result in larger checks for a longer period of time, resulting in higher lifetime benefits.

"Social Security benefits are designed to be actuarially equivalent for someone with average mortality," says certified financial planner Doug Lemons, retired deputy assistant regional commissioner with the Social Security Administration. "Theoretically, it should not make a difference when an individual begins collecting benefits. However, external factors may affect the actual amount of benefits received. These factors include (1) inflation as measured by annual cost-of-living increases, (2) the time value of money of taking benefits early and investing that amount, and (3) taxes."[8]

There is, indeed, a difference of opinion about when to claim, as some believe the life expectancies that the Social Security Administration uses are on the conservative side. It's best to take a middle-of-the-road approach, analyzing your own situation and deciding in favor of what makes sense financially and emotionally. For instance, if you are going to feel pinched by waiting a few extra months or a year until you turn 66 or beyond, or until 70, claim your benefits earlier.

Who benefits the most by waiting?

"We find that females, married couples, retirees who expect to invest in relatively conservative portfolios during retirement, and retirees who have longer life expectancies are likely to benefit most from delaying SS benefits," says David M. Blanchett, CFA, CFP, and head of retirement research for Morningstar's Investment Management group. "On the other hand, retirees who have shorter life expectancies or invest more aggressively and believe they can achieve a relatively high return on their retirement portfolios would likely be better off taking SS earlier."[9]

Figuring Out Your Potential Longevity

Of course, longevity is a factor. Before you look at the expenses and income you expect to have in retirement, think in terms of longevity. "The arc of life has lengthened," says Andrew Scott, coauthor of *The 100-Year Life: Living and Working in an Age of Longevity* and professor of economics at the London Business School. "We're fitter and healthier for longer. How long are you going to live? You have to think in terms of the future."[10]

For an estimate, you can use a life-expectancy calculator, such as the one on the Social Security Administration's website, at https://www.ssa.gov /OACT/population/longevity.html. Or you can begin by looking at how long your parents lived (or are living) and your own health. "Most people are going to live longer than their parents," Scott says.[11] The actuarial table on the SSA's website estimates that, as of this writing, men who are 65 today on average are expected to live to 84.0 and women to 86.6.[12]

Claim Later to Get a Larger Benefit Amount

Though 62 is one of the most popular times to begin claiming Social Security, waiting makes a difference, and each year you wait increases your monthly retirement benefit. For example, if your benefit will be $1,000 at your full retirement age of 66 and you opt to claim your Social Security at 62, your monthly check will be 75 percent of your full benefit amount, or $750. The amount grows each year based on a formula. According to the Society of Actuaries,

- if you postpone receipt of benefits from the age of 62 until you've turned 63, you will get 80 percent of your full benefit amount, or $800 monthly
- if you wait until you are 64 to receive benefits, you will get 87 percent, or $870 monthly
- and if you wait until you are 65, your benefit will be 93 percent, or $930 monthly,[13]

In short, you will receive approximately 5 percent more if you postpone onset of receipt from age 62 to age 63, 7 percent more if you wait from 63 until you are 64, 6 percent more if you postpone from 64 until 65, and 7 percent more from 65 to 66, for a total of 25 percent more between age 62 and full retirement, says Angela S. Deppe, coauthor of *It's Your Money! Simple Strategies to Maximize Your Social Security Income.*[14]

Increasing Your Benefit

If you wait past your full retirement age to begin your Social Security payouts, you'll increase your future Social Security check by approximately 8 percent each year. Using the same numbers, if you were to receive $1,000 a month at 66, by waiting one year you would receive

- $1,080 at 67
- $1,160 at 68
- $1,240 at 69
- and $1,320 at age 70.

"You suffer the most financially if you take it at 62," Deppe says. "You are penalized more than the benefit you receive if you go past 66."[15]

Though the increase is 8 percent each year from ages 66 to 70, the amount is not compounded, says Richard Johnson, director of the program on retirement policy at the Urban Institute, a nonpartisan research firm. Even waiting less than a year longer to claim your benefit makes a difference. "Every month that you delay, you get a little extra, from age 62 to 70," he says.[16]

Claiming as a Married Couple

If you're married, as you calculate when to claim your Social Security benefits, consider a future in which one of you dies before the other. If both of you have worked long enough to qualify for your own benefits, it's important that you coordinate when each of you will claim benefits. For married couples, it's particularly importantly for the higher earner to delay, because that amount becomes the survivor benefit for whoever lives longer, says Virginia P. Reno, former vice president for income security policy at the National Academy of Social Insurance, a research organization based in Washington, D.C. "Social Security is unique among pensions because it continues to have a larger payout for every year that you delay taking it," she says, adding that when it comes to nest eggs, most Americans ages 55 to 64 have a relatively small one, so will rely mostly on Social Security during retirement. The large majority of seniors count on Social Security for most of their income after age 65, and that has been the case for 30 years, she says.[17]

Reno is retired deputy commissioner for retirement and disability policy at the Social Security Administration.

If you wait until 70 or any other time after the earliest claiming age of 62, what resources will you and your spouse use to cover daily living expenses as well as health insurance premiums until you are eligible for Medicare at 65?

If you have savings or retirement accounts, some experts advise spending down funds rather than claiming Social Security early.

If you and your spouse are willing to speculate—that is, take an educated guess as to how long you will each live—you can create a plan. Of course, no one knows precisely how long they will live. That said, make an estimate, and begin to plan.

If the higher-earning person in a couple claims early, it can significantly lower the amount the surviving spouse receives. It's often better for the higher earner to wait as long as possible and at least until they turn 66, if not to 70. "For four out of every ten widows past 65, Social Security is all the income they have," says Anna Rappaport, chair of the Society of Actuaries Committee on Post-Retirement Needs and Risks. If you're a married couple, one person can claim early, and one can claim late, she adds.[18]

Claiming If You're Single

If you're able to claim Social Security later, it may be your best decision, especially if you're female, as women typically have higher life expectancies and typically have earned less than their male counterparts. Of course, this depends on your current health and other resources. Indeed, if your resources are limited, you may need to claim your Social Security at the earliest possible opportunity, which is at 62. If you're able to work, claiming later will give you a higher monthly benefit, as described above.

The decision concerning when to claim Social Security is a highly individual one. Some retirement specialists advise that if you're single you wait to claim as long as you can or wait until age 70. It's critical that you maximize your benefit by waiting until 70 if you can, as this may be the only—or at least the major—source of income you'll have in retirement, unless you have a pension, a significant amount of money in your 401(k) plan, or $400,000 in retirement savings, says Mary Hunt, author of *The Smart Woman's Guide to Planning for Retirement*.[19]

If you wait until 70 to take your Social Security and live another 20 years, you'll have a running start at having enough funds. "Keep in mind that these seriously rough figures do not allow for inflation or make any attempt to figure out what taxes will look like years or decades from now," Hunt adds.[20]

Suspending Social Security Benefits

There's another strategy to maximize your benefits that's not well known. Once you've reached your full retirement age (FRA), even if you have claimed early—for example, at 62 or some time before your FRA—you can suspend your benefits.

For example, at 65, you decide to claim your Social Security, taking your benefits a year before your FRA of 66. Your goal is to pay off credit debt carrying a 16 percent interest rate or higher.

Once you've paid off the debt, notify Social Security that you wish to suspend your benefits at the earliest opportunity, which is at your FRA of 66, if you were born between 1943 and 1954. For this plan, contact Social Security one month before your FRA to be placed on the voluntary suspension list effective the month you reach 66.[21]

The toll-free number for the Social Security Administration is 1 (800) 772-1213.

If you file before your FRA, you will get a reduced benefit. This means that any delayed retirement credits—8 percent per year—you receive after you suspend your benefit will be applied to your reduced benefit rather than to your full retirement benefit. In the case of filing at 65 and suspending at 66, you will lose the increased amount between 65 and 66, which is approximately 6.7 percent.[22] If you want to get out of debt before you retire, this strategy is an option.

Another reason to suspend is, for example, if you claimed at 62 not realizing your options. Once you reach your full retirement age of between 66 and 67, you can suspend until age 70, to earn what Social Security calls *delayed retirement credits* of 8 percent per year or as much as 32 percent.

FRA is the age at which you are able to claim your Social Security without receiving a reduced amount. As you will remember, if you claim your benefits at the earliest opportunity, which is age 62, you will receive a reduced amount, which is usually 25 percent less than your full benefit.

Yet some people feel they need the money at the earliest opportunity—or they actually do need the money. For example, someone might want to claim early because they want the money to travel, to pay for a child's wedding, or to pay off debt. Or they might need the money to pay the rent, feed and clothe themselves, or manage their health.

Knowing you have the option to suspend your benefits once you reach your full retirement age can help you decide when to claim.

Another reason to claim and suspend is if you lost your job at 62 and had planned on working longer. If you do land a job at 63, your only option is to withdraw your Social Security claim. If you withdraw, you must do it within 12 months of your initial claim, and you are required to pay back any benefits your received.[23]

This is different from suspending your benefits, which you are only allowed to do when you reach your FRA. Withdrawing is discussed more below.

The advantage of suspending your benefits is that you can gain 8 percent per year in additional benefits for those years after age 66, if that's your FRA. For example, say you decide to claim at 65 when you file for Medicare. You use the monthly payments to pay off a credit card balance at 16 percent or more. Or you use the money to take a 65th birthday celebration, a safari to Kenya.

You suspend your benefits on your 66th birthday and continue to accrue delayed retirement credits of 8 percent per year until you turn 70, when you max out on Social Security.

Suspending is an option, one that can help you with your retirement planning. If you'd prefer to be working between 62 and 66 or 70, you can claim your benefits at 62 and keep looking for work. Once you reach your FRA, if you've found a job, you can suspend your Social Security. Be sure to call and report that you've returned to work so SSA will stop sending you checks.

If You're Working or Want to Work

Since your Social Security benefits are calculated based on your 35 years with the highest income, you can increase your benefit amount by working extra years at a higher income, Rappaport says.[24] Say you're 55 or 60 and haven't worked 35 years yet or had a relatively low (or no) income in some years because you took off time to raise your children or care for your aging parents. If you have worked a considerable amount of time in one profession or field, you may be able to reenter the workplace at a higher salary than you've made in the past.

If you continue working, once you reach your full retirement age you can earn as much as you want and still receive your full Social Security check each month.[25] However, if you haven't yet reached your full retirement age of between 66 and 67 for those born after 1943, and you earn more than certain dollar amounts determined by Social Security for a particular year, some of your earnings will be withheld.[26] This is discussed in chapter 5.

There's really no reason to limit your earnings, because even though some benefits may be withheld, Social Security will pay you a higher monthly benefit when you reach your full retirement age. At that time, Social Security will recalculate your benefit so you receive credit for months you did not receive a benefit due to your earnings. As long as you continue to work and receive benefits, the SSA will check your record every year to see whether the extra earnings will increase your monthly benefit.[27]

Withdrawing Your Claim

There is another option for managing your Social Security benefits that is distinctly different from suspending your benefits: withdrawing your application. If you withdraw your application, which you can only do within the first year of your initial filing, you can later receive all of your benefits with no reductions. The catch is that you have to pay back all the money you received from Social Security in order to do this.[28]

Once you've decided when you might claim your Social Security retirement benefits, another key area to analyze is where to live in retirement. Read on to learn about staying where you are or finding a new home in retirement.

~

CHAPTER SEVEN

Aging in Place or Not

Housemates, Roommates, and More

Three-quarters of those 50 and older want to stay in their current home when they retire.[1] Yet almost four in ten retirees have moved since retiring.[2]

What is right for you depends on your personality, lifestyle, financial resources, relationships, and personal preferences on climate, activities, and proximity to friends and family.

If you want to lower your cost of living before or when you retire, finding ways to spend less on housing could be your single best strategy. If you are in your 50s, it's an ideal time to strategize about the next phase of your life. "Housing is absolutely the huge issue," says Jane Cullinane, author of several books on retirement, including *The Single Woman's Guide to Retirement.*[3]

There are a variety of ways to cut your housing costs as you approach retirement. One major way is to eliminate your mortgage. Even if you can pay it off, you'll still have to pay property taxes and insurance, and possibly homeowner's association dues or condominium common charges. If your building's board hasn't stockpiled a reserve for capital improvements, you might be faced with a monthly or yearly assessment for capital improvements. Factor all of this into your housing costs as you plan for the time when your paycheck is gone.[4]

As you head toward retirement, consider three primary options: aging in place, relocating, and downsizing nearby. Many people equate self-worth with the home they own and find it difficult to consider selling, says Mary Hunt, author of *The Smart Woman's Guide to Planning for Retirement: How to Save for Your Future Today.* Most people "slip into denial," she says. It can take a "cataclysmic event" to push you to evaluate your situation, Cullinane says. Maybe you've lost a job, faced unforeseen medical expenses, or begun to realize that your expenses are too high to allow a comfortable lifestyle.[5]

Eliminating Your Mortgage

Some people strip the equity out of their home by refinancing and taking cash out for a European cruise, an in-ground pool, or college tuition and then find themselves with little or no equity. "They've spent their future," Hunt says. "You've got to get rid of your mortgage."[6]

Hunt, who has been writing the newsletter *Debt-Proof Living* since 1992, sold the house she and her husband had lived in for 27 years. At first, they thought they would refinance the Orange County, California, home to get a lower interest rate. But, at that time, the mortgage payment was just too high, at $2,000 a month plus property taxes and insurance. "We started to face the truth, and age"—she was born in 1948—"and it all collided. We knew what we had to do. We have to sell this house. We can't afford it." So they did, leaving enough cash for them to move almost anywhere in the country. They chose Erie, Colorado, halfway between Boulder and Denver, where they bought a less expensive house with all cash.[7]

Relocating

If you have equity in your home and are open to relocating to a less expensive market, you can realize significant savings, and your financial life will be easier, experts advise.

Consider several factors when thinking about relocation. The social and psychological aspects of your life contribute to your decisions. "We have 'Peter Pan' houses, and we think we're never going to get older," Cullinane says. "The status quo is easier, to do nothing than to do something." In today's mobile society, some people like Cullinane who have moved multiple times may no longer feel attached to a particular place. "We had lost our roots" traveling and living in different places and "found it very energizing and invigorating to start over," she says. For example, she and her husband moved from Cincinnati, Ohio, to Hammock Beach, Florida, a planned community.[8]

In thinking about whether to stay or move, the first step is to consider what is most important to you. Here are some questions to ask yourself:

- Do you want to lower your cost of living even if you don't completely retire?

- How does the cost of living where you live compare to the places you are considering?
- Are you still working either in a full-time job with benefits or in some other way, such as running your own business or professional practice?
- Is it important to you to be near family members who live elsewhere?
- Is the climate where you live appealing to you, or do you prefer to explore other climates?
- Do you want more space, less space, a different kind of space?
- Does an active-lifestyle community appeal to you?
- Do you or your partner need assisted living?
- Do you prefer a continuing-care retirement community (CCRC)?

In making a move, Cullinane says, consider transportation, medical care, political and religious life, and universal design—which is a set of principles that makes your home easy to access and live in no matter your age, size, or abilities. In addition, if you are already 65 and receiving Medicare, make sure the primary care doctor you plan to see when you relocate accepts Medicare.[9]

Know Your Priorities

The clearer you are on your preferences, the smoother this part of your life will be. If you are still working, begin thinking about what else you would like to do besides work.

Among the first things to consider, experts say, is how you would like to live the next part of your life. This is a time to reflect on where you have been and where you would like to go.[10]

- If you have not traveled, do you wish to travel, or do you wish to travel more than you already have?
- Do you want to spend more time with family members, including grown children and grandchildren?
- If you don't have children, do you want to live near other relatives or friends?
- What type of living arrangement do you prefer? Single family home? Condominium or co-op? Cohousing? Active-adult or lifestyle community? Continuing-care retirement community?
- Do you want a more flexible schedule so you can pursue other interests, such as golf, tennis, pickleball, skiing, hiking, painting, or fishing?
- Do you simply want more control over your time?
- Do you prefer a more relaxed pace than the one you have now?

- Do you want time to renovate your home or declutter your home to prepare it for sale?
- Do you want to explore other locations where you might live in retirement?
- Is your home comfortable now, and will it be in the future? For example, are you able to climb stairs? Are you able to step into the bathtub or shower?

Snowbirds

Whether you stay in the home you've lived in for many years depends on a number of factors, among them your finances. Though finances aren't necessarily your first consideration, they are an integral part of your decision. For example, if your mortgage is paid off and you have a pension, savings, and Social Security, you may want to live in two places during the year. Perhaps, if you live in a four-season climate, you'll want to become a snowbird, flying south when the temperature cools. A couple in their 70s alternates between their single-family suburban Michigan home and a South Florida condominium they bought more than 30 years ago. He is still working, and she spends three weeks to a month at a time in Florida, and he joins her when he can. They maintain Michigan as their primary residence and enjoy living in two places. Two of their three grown children and their families live in others states, and they visit them as well.

Downsizing

For others, downsizing and staying in the same area has been the answer in retirement. Downsizing is not just a physical change. Sometimes it's a way to create a new life in a new space.[11]

Retired or semiretired couples sometimes prefer to stay in the area in which they have lived for many years, downsizing from a single-family home to a condominium. Sometimes they lower their cost of living, yet in some markets in the United States—such as the Washington, D.C., area—downsizing can mean financial upsizing.[12]

If money isn't an obstacle, downsizing from a suburban area to a more urban area or from a single-family home to a condominium in the same area can be smooth.

In addition, if your mortgage is paid off, it will be even easier.

Kaye and Edward downsized from their single-family home of 33 years to a two-bedroom, two-bath condominium just two miles away. By moving, they are trading stairs and mowing the lawn for less space and more amenities, including indoor and outdoor swimming pools. They preferred not to uproot themselves and pared down their possessions one step at a time. They traded a backyard for "communal living." For the couple living in the Washington, D.C., area, the move was, according to Edward, a "new adventure, far more positive than negative."[13]

Sometimes the new property is nearby but considerably smaller and less expensive. That was the case for Howard and Paige, who sold their five-bedroom suburban house for a suburban two-bedroom condominium.[14]

Finding a New Home

In making a move, ask yourself,

- Do you want a one-level condominium or a one-level single-family home?
- Would a multilevel, single-family house with a master bedroom on the first floor work?
- Do you prefer new construction or older real estate?
- Do you want to live in a townhouse with an elevator or one in which an elevator can be installed?
- Are you able to find a place you can afford near your family or friends?

Howard and Paige wanted to be near their grown children and grandchildren, so staying in the Washington, D.C., area suited them. They wanted to avoid stairs at home as much as possible and preferred to spend less than $600,000 to $800,000.

They preferred three bedrooms but settled on two with a small outdoor space for a garden.[15]

If you have decided you are going to downsize, here are some tips:

- Figure out whether you're going to buy or sell first or both simultaneously. If you can carry the cost of two properties at the same time, you can relocate without having to rent in between.
- Consider how far you want to be from public transportation—either a bus or subway line or other shuttle service.
- If you're trying to spend less on housing, search for properties in areas adjacent to your ideal location, as prices may be lower for similar properties.[16]

- Consider working with a professional—an organizer or interior designer or a senior move manager through the National Association of Senior Move Managers.

Relocating to a Different Area

If you prefer to move to a different geographical area to be near family and friends or for the weather or a combination of factors, the financial aspect of your relocation is likely to take more time and research than if you were to move locally.

In considering a long-distance move, ask yourself,

- Is your mortgage paid off on your current home?
- What is the difference in the cost of living between your current location and the places you are considering?
- Will you need to obtain a mortgage in your new location?
- What will property taxes be like in a new home? If you don't have school-age children, do you need a town with great schools but higher taxes?
- If the new location costs more, will you have adequate resources to cover your expenses comfortably?
- Will you want or need to work in the new location?
- If so, what is the job market like in places you are considering?
- Is there state income tax? What is the sales tax like?

If you decide to move to another state for whatever combination of reasons, evaluate your financial situation carefully, and research the locations you are considering.

Mike and Barbara ultimately sold their Bethesda, Maryland, home of 26 years. First, they spent time deciding where they wanted to move. Next, they analyzed their financial situation. "It's a lot of money locked up in the house," says Barbara, who was 63 at the time we spoke and had retired from her job as a lobbyist two years before. Wanting to avoid the mid-Atlantic winters, the couple considered moving to Hawaii, where they had lived while Mike was in the US Navy, but decided it was too far for their grown children to visit regularly. They also thought of San Diego, Savannah, Georgia, and Charleston, South Carolina, but ultimately decided on Florida. Through friends they learned of a new community near Jacksonville where they would buy property and have a single-family home built. If necessary, they would rent a place in the interim. Because the new home cost less than the house they were selling, they would have cash to spare.[17]

Family Connections and Social Networks

If living near grandchildren, grown children, siblings, or other relatives or friends is important during this part of your life, analyze whether relocating is practical.

- Consider the nature of the relationship with your grown children. Regardless of how good it is, figure out your boundaries and how you would create a life of your own if you were to move near them.
- Think about how you would spend your time in the new location. Would you seek part-time work or take classes so you are not dependent solely on family members to occupy your time and energy?
- Be aware of leaving long-time friends and possible community support. Consider how you would establish new relationships.
- Analyze the financial aspects of relocating. For example, if you have more than one child and more than one grandchild and moving interests you, compare the cost in each area with where you live now.[18]

Health, Safety, and Comfort

If you're like a lot of people—the approximately 60 percent of Americans in retirement who don't relocate—staying in the home you've lived in for many years can be appealing. If you're not going to find a new place to live either nearby or far away, think about universal design, Jane Cullinane says. Will you be able to climb the stairs in your current home? If it's possible, can you afford to install an elevator? "Whether you decide to move or stay, find ways to make your home easy to access no matter what your age, size or abilities," she says.[19]

Options include

- a first-floor master bedroom and bath
- nonskid flooring
- curbless showers
- task lighting in the kitchen and other work areas
- bathroom grab bars
- lever- or pedal-controlled faucet handles
- an entryway ramp

- covered carports and boarding spaces
- and well-lit hallways.[20]

Going Solo

If you're on your own at this time in your life and financial considerations are a concern, housemates can be an option.

Since housing costs typically consume a third or more of living expenses for people 55 and older, sharing living space is often driven by economics.[21]

The desire for companionship can be another motivation. The perceived security of a housemate arrangement can drive the search for "aging in community" as a viable alternative to growing older alone or in a more traditional situation such as marriage.[22]

Sometimes it's the wish to remain in the community or home lived in for many years that drives the decision. "Not everyone can live together well," says Kirby Dunn, executive director of HomeShare, Vermont, an organization that has helped people find housemates for more than 30 years. "It does require a certain amount of flexibility on both people's part. It's a little bit of a dance that you have to do."[23]

Finding a compatible and secure situation isn't easy. Yet it can be worth the time and effort. "We weren't intended to drive into the garage and turn on the TV," says Marianne Kilkenny, who founded an organization called Women for Living in Community. Kilkenny advises knowing yourself as a key to finding compatible housemates. "You have to do your internal work. Identify what you want first."[24]

Safety and Security

For safety and security reasons, when considering any shared housing arrangement, background checks and references are essential. Then the success depends on how well the people can get along in shared space. Among the chief issues that can surface in shared housing arrangements is the ability to continue to pay. A former human resource professional, Kilkenny has relied on her interviewing skills to evaluate potential candidates. For example, if a prospective housemate mentions plans to help an adult child with a down payment on a house, she asks how that might affect her ability to pay rent. She also uses "behavioral interviewing" to uncover hidden attitudes or situations that would disqualify someone. Some organized home-share programs suggest a trial period of two weeks or longer to decide whether a match is suitable.[25]

It's wise to consider the kind of agreement made for payment, the length of the agreement, and plans for ending an arrangement in case it's not working.

To find a suitable sharing situation, rely on personal contacts first. Beyond that, organizations such as the National Shared Housing Resource Center, which lists agencies throughout the country, can help.[26]

Read more about this in Chapter 10.

Think carefully about where you will be comfortable living in retirement or semiretirement. Evaluate your resources carefully so you make decisions that you won't have to change. It can be costly to move again. The better you know what you want, the smoother your transition will be. If you decide that relocating meets your needs, take time to select a place that will be affordable for the long run. If you sell the home you have lived in for many years, you can use the money to find a place with a lower cost of living. Read on to find out how.

CHAPTER EIGHT

~

Using Your Home to Fund Your Dream Retirement Adventure

Whether you are financially well prepared for retirement or not, using the equity in your home to help fund your retirement lifestyle can be an option. If you don't have a mortgage, you're in the best position with the most flexibility.

More than a third (37 percent) of baby boomers have not considered their options for retiring, according to a January 2020 survey of the National Association of Personal Financial Advisors. Among Generation X, 54 percent have not thought about their retirement options.[1] And that means they may be holding on to homes that could help them to retire sooner than they might think they can.

Selling a mortgage-free house can put money in your pocket and give you the opportunity to dream and explore. If you have considerable equity in your home and prefer to live in a different location, that equity may just be enough to get you a mortgage-free home in a warmer climate, with lower taxes and a high quality of living. You can't guess. You have to do the footwork to discover where you might want to live, whether you'll be comfortable relocating, and how much it will cost. If you've moved more than once in your life, you know what it takes. You might consider consulting a financial expert who can run scenarios that include selling your house versus keeping it and how that factors into your retirement finances.

Even if you are still carrying a mortgage, if you have equity in your home—say, 60 percent or more—selling can still be a route to a new retirement lifestyle. The biggest advantage, according to some who have made the change, is the sense of freedom that lies ahead.[2] Some like the idea of selling their current home first, giving them the option to rent while their new home is being built or while deciding where to buy. The calculations necessary to trade one home for another are highly individual and depend on the value of the original home, the equity it has, anticipated retirement income and future expenses.[3]

Yet if you are mortgage-free, you'll have even more options, because any money you clear in the sale goes directly into your pocket after real estate agent fees and other costs associated with real estate sales. "If you can be retired and not have a mortgage, it can be a lot better," says Anna Rappaport, chair of the Society of Actuaries Committee on Post-Retirement Needs and Risks.[4] Without a monthly mortgage payment, your housing cost in retirement will be lower. You will still have to pay property taxes and, if, for example, you purchase a condominium or move to an active adult community, monthly common charges and possibly assessments.

Freeing Up Money

Selling a fully paid-off home that no longer meets your needs or wants can free up money for the purchase of a less expensive, more suitable home and, possibly, a mortgage-free lifestyle.[5]

Consider JanSuzanne and Paul, who had paid off their mortgage and were willing to take on some risk. In 2012 they sold their suburban New York home and left for Israel, where they rented an apartment for 10 months. Next they spent a month traveling in southern Africa and Europe and then rented an apartment in Manhattan for two months. They had sold most of their possessions except for personal memorabilia and ultimately bought a furnished condominium in South Florida for cash. "By moving to a less-expensive area, it frees up money to travel," says JanSuzanne, who is now in her mid-70s. She and her husband had been in business for many years and felt they had enough money to feel secure and wanted to live closer to relatives already living in Florida. Family relationships, the climate, and the cost of living drove their decision. "The rest didn't matter," she says. "Nothing will be perfect. We prioritized."[6]

Another couple, Phyllis and Joseph, now in their 70s, also bought a place in Florida a few years ago. Though they still had a mortgage on their northeast home where they had lived for 27 years, selling it gave them enough money to buy a mortgage-free place.[7]

Biggest Asset

Since your home may be your biggest asset in creating a new retirement lifestyle, consider how you want to live now and for the foreseeable future. Unless you are willing to relocate more than once, which can be costly, consider your income and expenses as you move forward. Not everyone either has a clear idea of what they want or is willing to rent temporarily and live in several places before purchasing a home. Sometimes people have an idea, but it changes or evolves over time. Remember, for most people, the phase of life that has been called retirement can last 25 or 30 years.

Some people on the brink of retirement have made decisions or have begun a new lifestyle with the disclaimer, "If we don't like it, we can move back" or "If my lifestyle becomes too expensive, I can sell my home and downsize."

All of this is true, but multiple moves can be costly in terms of real estate transaction fees and potential emotional upheaval. The better you know yourself and what you like, the less likely you will have to keep rethinking or changing your plan.

There are many different ways to use the equity in your home for retirement. Here are three:

- Downsize to less expensive housing in your area, and invest any remaining money from the sale of your home.
- Downsize to less expensive housing in a less expensive housing market, and invest the rest of the money from the sale of your original home.
- Move to an active-adult community in a less expensive area, and invest the rest of the money from the sale of your home.

Traditionally there are two ways to calculate the cost of living in retirement, experts say. The first is the assumption that you will need 75 to 80 percent of your preretirement gross income. The second is to create a budget.[8]

The first approach doesn't factor in whether you have paid off your mortgage, if you intend to sell your house and downsize, if you plan to relocate to a less expensive market, and the kind of lifestyle you prefer.

Creating a budget or more than one considers different variables and combinations. It is a "spending plan going forward," says Anna Rappaport. "Are you going to move, or are you going to stay put?" Downsizing can save you 35 percent or more on housing costs, she adds. "You really need to think about the long run."[9]

Are You Ready?

When you consider using your home to fund your retirement, figure out if starting a new life in a different space in a new location is for you. Among the nearly four in ten retirees who moved, 34 percent said they wanted to reduce expenses, 33 percent said their goal was to downsize to a smaller space, and 22 percent said they wanted to start a new chapter in life.[10] Whatever motivates you to sell your home, ask yourself these questions:

- Can you view this time in your life as an opportunity? A time to think about things you've always wanted to do? Places you've wanted to visit? Something you've wanted to buy? If so, selling your home can free up money and create a new lifestyle that will cost less.[11]
- How do you feel about your current home? Are you prepared to donate, sell, or toss many of your possessions?
- Does the idea of a new chapter in life seem appealing? Liberating? Intimidating? Overwhelming?
- Would the opportunity to pare down and eliminate clutter be a relief? A burden? Too much upheaval?

Spending Plan

Before taking any concrete steps, analyze your current and future finances. Calculate what your income is likely to be and the sources of that income.[12]

Do you have a defined benefit pension with a fixed amount of income each month and Social Security? Or will you be relying on money from your 401(k) plan, which is less certain than a fixed monthly income from a pension? Review chapter 2, "Evaluating Your Resources: Creating a Budget," and chapter 6, "When to Claim Social Security: Maximizing Your Monthly Check."

After you downsize, your cost of living may be lower, but be sure to include these items in your retirement spending plan:

- home maintenance and repairs
- vehicle maintenance and repairs
- travel and entertainment costs
- the potential for rising health-care costs

Preparing to Sell Your Home

Selling your home of many years requires planning. A good first step is to determine how much your current home is worth. You can estimate or consult a real estate agent or more than one, but a professional appraisal will reveal how much your home is worth in the current market. A useful source is the National Association of Appraisers,[13] which focuses on real estate appraisals. You will have a more precise idea of how much your home—whether a single-family house, townhouse, or condominium—is worth. Another source is the American Society of Appraisers.[14]

A real estate broker can complete a comparative market analysis (CMA) for your property using comparable properties. Ideally the comparables should be properties with the same number of bedrooms and baths, be located within a quarter-mile of your home, and be within 200 square feet of the size of your home. Real estate markets can change quickly, so be sure the data used is no older than six months.[15]

When you are actually selling your home, mortgage lenders require an appraisal before they'll provide a loan. The property must appraise for the full sale price of the house or more, otherwise the lender will not approve a loan for the property.[16]

Where to Go

People often choose a place close to family and friends, where they own a second home, or where they have spent time on vacation. Wherever you consider moving, it's not the same as visiting or vacationing there. The weather will vary by season and will not necessarily be what you experienced in spring or summer. In addition, with weather patterns changing in recent years, find out as much as you can about the recent climate in any potential location. Research online, speak to people who live in that area, and be realistic about how a great climate in the winter can be unbearable in the heat and humidity of summer. No location will be perfect. Unless moving at different times of the year—becoming a snowbird—appeals to you (and you can afford it), find one place that meets your top three criteria.

One of those will likely be affordability—the main reason, if not one of the three main reasons, you are relocating in the first place.

For example, if you know you want to leave the Washington, D.C., area for San Antonio, you can just focus on neighborhoods in San Antonio. If you can afford to travel to the new location at least once before you move, you can save time and avoid mistakes in the long run. "The faster you can make the right decision, the better off you are," says Sylvia Ehrlich, president of Intrepid Relocation International.[17]

Many people research online first, make appointments with real estate salespersons or brokers, speak by phone, and then travel to see as many places as they can in a limited time. Some people—the tech-savvy—even use Face-Time to view places or share them with spouses or partners. Indeed, this is not a method for everyone.

Approximately a third of those who bought a home between 2018 and 2019 were ages 54 to 72, according to the April 2019 *Home Buyer and Seller Generational Trends Report.*[18]

The source of the down payment was proceeds from the sale of a primary residence. Among those ages 54 to 63, more than half (51 percent) used the proceeds for the down payment. Among those ages 64 to 72, more than half (54 percent) did. The percentage was the highest among those ages 73 to 93 at 60 percent.[19] The report did not specify how large the down payment was.

Whatever route you decide to take, make sure you will have adequate resources for your other retirement expenses. Whether or not you decide to purchase a home in retirement will depend on your total financial picture. In making your decisions, considering your finances is essential, yet think beyond to the kind of living situation that will feel comfortable for you. One widow in her late 70s opted to sell her home and pay a monthly fee in an independent-living community rather than purchase a condominium or a home in a different independent-living or continuing-care retirement community. She opted to invest her money with the assistance of a trusted financial expert who helped her create quarterly streams of income from the sale of her mortgage-free suburban home. Another couple from California in their mid- to late 60s opted to rent in a luxury building in Chevy Chase, Maryland. They had sold their home and relocated to be near their adult children and grandchildren. They liked the flexibility of renting. Your decision will be entirely personal, based on your assets and individual preferences.

Extra Expenses

If you decide to purchase a condominium, townhouse, or other property in an active-adult or other type of community, be sure to consider any common charges that typically will increase each year. In addition, check if there is a reserve fund and if it is funded for any community you are considering, or have your lawyer do it. Ask a financial person at the property rather than the marketing director if there are any assessments pending.

Honest Evaluation

It's important to be as honest with yourself (and your spouse or partner) as possible. The earlier you plan, the better. Even if you are in the 55-to-64-age range, there is still time to plan the future. Your approach can be, "How can I readjust my lifestyle so that I can afford it?" Anna Rappaport says.[20]

No matter where you decide to live, the sooner you consider how you might handle your real estate assets, the better prepared you will be. Perhaps you don't need to sell your home to help finance your retirement. Maybe you don't need the money but no longer wish to take care of a home of your own. Or maybe you will need to sell in order to fund the kind of retirement you prefer. Whatever your situation, looking at the bigger picture, getting input from a financial expert and a real estate agent, and considering your preferences will help give you a sense of the option that is right for you. Read on to learn about different kinds of places to live in retirement.

~

CHAPTER NINE

Housing Options Other than Your Long-Term Home

Once you've decided to sell your long-term home, the next step is to consider where you're going to live instead. In chapter 7, we discussed whether to stay in place, downsize nearby, or relocate to be near family or friends. Beyond where you are going to live geographically, what kind of space and amenities appeal to you, and which are affordable? How important are peers?

When considering a move, ask yourself,

- What kind of environment appeals to you?
- What are your needs and lifestyle preferences?
- What can you afford now and in the future?

"Know yourself," says Susanne Matthiesen, former managing director of aging services at CARF International, an organization based in Tucson that accredits services for older people. She is assistant vice president, accreditation operations at the National Committee for Quality Assurance, a nonprofit in Washington, D.C. "Know where you want to live," she says. "Are you the kind of person who is looking to be in a community with peers?"[1]

Before making any decisions, ask yourself,

- How important is it to be near family members?
- Is a warm climate or are four seasons preferable?
- Are lawn, garden, and landscaping services essential?
- Do you want to live in or near an urban center?

- Are amenities like indoor and outdoor swimming pools, scheduled activities and clubs, tennis or pickleball courts, a nearby golf course, walking trails, or a lake or other body of water important?

Make a written list of your priorities.

By speaking to family members and friends, you may learn of places you hadn't considered. Overall, though, it's your life, so make sure your needs and wants will be met.

Active-Adult or Lifestyle Communities

When Jacquie of Leesburg, Virginia, retired early at 56 from a job because she faced a 45-mile one-way commute when the federal agency relocated, she was ready for a change. Though she volunteered at her church and at Habitat for Humanity, she missed the camaraderie at work. "Everybody else was still working," she says. So she began searching for places to move and found Trilogy at Lake Frederick in Lake Frederick, Virginia. She did not want to move to Florida, and, after two or three visits to Trilogy she found property overlooking a lake where she could build a new home. "Being alone, this is so much more comfortable than moving to a whole new area," she says.[2]

A 55-plus active-adult community located in the foothills of the Blue Ridge Mountains, approximately a 90-minute drive from Washington, D.C., Jacquie's new community has homes of different sizes, a farm-to-table restaurant, and an athletic club. In addition, there are indoor and outdoor pools, walking trails, a community garden, billiards and other games, an art studio, and pickleball and tennis courts.

Tom and Kathy decided to sell their Colonial house on three acres in Gaithersburg, Maryland, and find something smaller on less land. "We wanted to be active, meet new people, and have a lot of activities," says Tom, who had retired at 59. They ultimately moved to a new home at Symphony Village, an active-adult community in Centreville, Maryland. They wanted to be within an hour of their two daughters. Kathy had worked as a nurse, and Tom worked as a manager at a telecommunications company for many years. He enjoys golf, and she plays tennis, so both would find what they wanted at Symphony Village.[3]

Analyze the Finances

If you consider moving to an active-adult or lifestyle community, analyze the finances. "It's a major decision and a huge investment," Susanne Matthiesen says. "You really have to tour the place carefully, make multiple visits." Determine how fiscally sound the community is. Ask to see the organization's most recent audit or annual financial report, and speak to the person in charge of the community's finances. Avoid relying on the community's marketing person, who may have limited information about the organization's finances, Matthiesen adds.[4]

Evaluate your resources to determine if moving to an active lifestyle community is a good financial decision.

Intangibles

Once you sort out the financial side of the decision, determine how comfortable you are with the place or places you are considering, Matthiesen says.[5] Ask yourself,

- What would it actually be like to live there?
- What is the culture of the place?
- What are the demographics?
- Is the atmosphere vibrant and active?
- Does it have the activities you like?
- Is it tied to a university?

Moving to a community can be the answer to where to live during the transition to retirement, in retirement, or even if you are still working part-time. It may or may not be an age-restricted community. That's up to you.

Active-Adult Communities versus Continuing-Care Retirement Communities

Research thoroughly any place you are considering, whether it is an active-adult community—also known as a lifestyle community—or a continuing-care retirement community (CCRC). The major difference between an active-adult community and a CCRC is that an active-adult community usually does not include any centralized dining or health-care options. There may be restaurants in the community. In contrast, a CCRC typically includes independent-living options, assisted-living accommodations, and some kind of health-care component, Matthiesen says.[6] For a state-by-state list of CCRCs, visit https://findcontinuingcare.com/.

Active-adult communities are distinct from CCRCs in that a CCRC offers a "tiered approach," with independent living, assisted living, often some type of nursing care, and sometimes a separate Alzheimer's wing.[7]

Unless they have chronic health issues, those in their late 50s to mid-70s who prefer to live in a community typically choose an active community, not a CCRC.

Sometimes those in their 80s choose to live in a place that offers continuing care. Often younger adults choose active-adult communities, which are "no different than any other planned community, expect there is an age requirement," says Margaret A. Wylde, president and chief executive of the ProMatura Group, a market research firm in Oxford, Mississippi.[8] Typically a certain percentage of the residents must be 55 or older. Whether you choose an active-adult community or a CCRC likely depends on your health status and personal preferences.

Since emerging in 2019 and spreading worldwide in 2020, the coronavirus pandemic has not changed the costs or financial risks found in these communities, but it has brought a new set of risks into focus, according to a 2020 report by the Society of Actuaries. "COVID-19 could change the view that these organizations are safe and very desirable places to age," says the report. "While infectious diseases have long been a risk, COVID-19 presents extreme risk to the residents of these communities, and it brings a spotlight to the related issues. The variation in the way different communities have responded indicates that residents may face very different situations. Such communities remain an important option for seniors, but they involve a complex set of risks and require thoughtful consideration of the trade-offs before they are selected. More consumer protection and disclosure would help consumers make more informed choices."[9]

Some active-adult communities set the requirement at age 62 and older. In addition, 80 percent of the residences must be occupied by those in the specific age range, as regulated by the Fair Housing Amendments Act and the Housing for Older Persons Act. The majority of active-adult communities—85 to 90 percent—are comprised of single-family homes, while the rest are condominiums or rental apartments. Active-adult communities typically attract those ages 60 to 65, some retired and others still working but considering retirement. Ninety-five percent purchase their homes or condominiums, prepare their own meals, and have the choice of participating in group activities at a clubhouse or community center. People who opt for an active-adult community are typically downsizing and want a home with amenities and services such as lawn care and snow shoveling.[10]

Those in their 80s are more likely to move to independent living or assisted living, which may or may not be part of a CCRC. The average age for entering independent living is 82, Wylde says.[11]

Finding the Right Place

Once you've found a community you like through personal recommendations or an Internet search or both, visit several times to determine whether or not it will meet your needs and be a place you would enjoy. Here are a few things to consider:

- How well are the houses constructed?
- How safe and secure is the community?
- How accessible are the homes for the disabled and the elderly?
- Would you enjoy having the other residents as neighbors?
- Are younger family members permitted to visit?

"Talk to the people who live there," Matthiesen says.[12] Most communities have open houses or will arrange a tour or a two or three-night stay for a reasonable per-night or package rate. In addition, if you are relocating to a different area to live in an active-lifestyle community or a CCRC, visit the surrounding community to determine the available services. If it's an active-lifestyle community, research what kind of medical care is available nearby. If you have reached 65, make sure you can find a medical practice that accepts Medicare. Find out if there is a shuttle bus or other transportation to basic services including supermarkets, drugstores, hardware stores, restaurants, and cultural and arts activities. Chapter 11 discusses how to get around if you can no longer drive.

When selecting a community, experts and residents of active-adult communities offer the following advice:

- Check out the atmosphere at the amenities, including the clubhouse, indoor and outdoor pools, tennis courts, entertainment, kayaking, art studio, and walking trails.
- Drive through the community first, and then visit the sales center. If you have friends who live in a community, arrange a meeting.
- Find out how much the homeowners' association fee is and whether it includes Internet, utilities, and lawn and landscaping services.
- Determine, to the extent that you can, whether the residents are people with whom you would enjoy socializing. Or are you going to use your

home in the adult community as a home base and socialize mostly with family and friends outside the community? Wylde says to ask yourself, "Is it a community of like-minded people?"[13]

- Consider how much privacy appeals to you in your everyday life. Are you willing to trade some privacy for community activities and neighbors who could become friends? Not everyone is suited to community living and may find it's like living in a fishbowl. Be honest with yourself about your needs and preferences. Keep in mind that as the years go on you may appreciate the safety, security, and camaraderie a community can offer.

Admission to a CCRC

If you have a chronic health problem or your spouse or partner does, you may want to consider moving to a CCRC at a younger age. Also, if you don't want to move again later in life, a CCRC may be for you. Before admission, residents are often evaluated to make sure they are able to live in the independent-living area. "Some CCRCs may require a health screening at the time of admission," Matthiesen says. "Some facilities may require the applicant's health records and a physical exam."[14]

Costs of a CCRC

If you're considering a CCRC, the cost varies by region and the size of the home you choose. Housing costs tend to be similar to the median housing prices in the area. Typically, residents pay an entrance fee and a monthly fee thereafter.[15]

Most often, residents sell their home as a way to afford the entrance; CCRCs have several different types of contracts, so read any contract carefully, and seek legal or financial advice before signing, Matthiesen advises. In addition, check with the Department of Insurance in the state in which the CCRC is located to determine how the CCRC is licensed. Determine the age of the residents; as the population ages, costs can increase, potentially creating financial risks.[16] Entrance fees are typically at least $100,000 to approximately $400,000 and depend on the CCRC's location, the size of the home, the level of care at the time you enter, and the CCRC agreement, a legal document.

When considering a CCRC, ask the following questions:

- Which services are included in the monthly fee, and which cost extra?
- Are inspection reports available for your review?
- When you move or pass away, is any part of the entry fee refundable?[17]

Entrance fees are usually structured in one of three ways, according to CARF's *Consumer Guide to Understanding Financial Performance and Reporting in Continuing Care Retirement Communities*: (1) *Declining-scale refunds* can decline at the rate of 1 percent each month, so after six months, the refund would be 94 percent of the entrance fee. (2) Using *partially refundable entrance fees*, the CCRC guarantees a specific percentage to be refunded within a certain period of time—sometimes 50 percent or as high as 90 percent upon moving out or passing away. In case of death, the resident's estate receives the refund. (3) With a *full refund*, the entrance fee will be refunded, though a fixed charge may be deducted before the refund is given.[18] Typically, the living space must be reoccupied before any refund is given.

With long-term residence and care in the same community, residents can still face risk. For example, according to the Government Accountability Office, financial difficulties at a CCRC can mean unexpected increases in monthly fees or the loss of all or some of the entrance fee.[19]

Your Choice

If you are in your mid-50s to your mid to late 60s and are in good health, whether to move to an active-lifestyle community is your choice. If you wait until you are older and no longer feel comfortable in your own home, you may forfeit the choice, but even then there are other options available to you. There are retirement communities that are not active-adult communities or CCRCs. CCRCs are typically regulated by the state in which they are located, while other communities are not. Some offer independent living only or a combination of independent living and assisted living and are not classified as CCRCs. Some allow you to pay a monthly fee and do not require an up-front entrance fee. Whatever type of place you consider, check its financial status. In addition, factor in future annual increases in monthly fees, and consider whether you will be able to afford those based on your retirement income.

If you don't make a decision on your own, someone else—grown children, for example—may become involved. Generally, it's better to make decisions to move when you are younger and will find it easier to execute the move.

In your 60s, "there's a lot of life left," says gerontologist Mary Kay Buysse, executive director of the National Association of Senior Move Managers, a membership organization that helps manage the downsizing and relocation process. "At 88, there's less of a choice," she says. Having a choice is central to the success of your move.[20]

Figuring out which location is right for your retirement depends on cost-of-living in a locale including taxes, climate, and other factors. Chapter 10 discusses how to determine the right location for you.

~

CHAPTER TEN

Choosing Your Dream Location

Deciding Where to Live

Where you live in retirement is an entirely personal decision. Knowing yourself will make it easier to find the right place. Research shows that about four in ten retirees relocate in retirement while the rest stay in place.[1] If you are not sure where you want to live in retirement, read on.

People tend to relocate for a variety of reasons. The largest percentage —34 percent—moved to reduce their cost of living. Thirty-three percent downsized to a smaller home. Other reasons included the 27 percent who moved to be closer to family and friends, the 23 percent who relocated for a better climate, and the 22 percent who moved to start a new chapter.[2]

Choosing Your Location

The first step in figuring out where to live is to consider your priorities. Ask yourself,

- Do you want to lower your cost of living?
- Do you need or want less living space?
- Will you be working part-time, full-time, or not at all?
- What other activities will be part of your life?
- Do you have volunteer work that you will continue in retirement?
- Do you have interests or hobbies that you want to rekindle?

- Which relationships are most important to you? Adult children? Grandchildren? Siblings? Other relatives? Close friends? Meeting new people? Making new friends?
- How important is climate? Do you want to live in a place with four seasons, or is getting away from the cold or heat a priority?
- Do you have a vacation home that could become your primary residence in retirement?
- Is there a place you have vacationed that would be appealing and affordable during retirement?
- Which other locations appeal to you and your spouse or partner?
- How does the cost of living in those other locations compare with the cost of where you are living now?
- How important is it that you live near an airport—or at least reasonably close to one?
- Is living near or within walking distance of a place of worship important to you?
- Is living near an urban center a priority?
- Do you want or need to be able to use public transportation now or in the future?
- Is living near a university or a community college of interest?
- Is access to a fitness center important?
- Can you find a doctor who bills Medicare, or are you still using other insurance?
- How close do you want to be to a highly rated hospital or academic health center?

There are numerous lists of the best places to live in retirement that rank states and cities according to a variety of factors. These can certainly be useful—or at least interesting. Yet your own personal assessment can be more important, because even if a place ranks high, as Nebraska did on a Bankrate. com survey for 2019,[3] it may not fit any of your criteria. The criteria for the Bankrate.com rankings were affordability, crime, culture, weather, and wellness. While these are worthwhile considerations, it's important that you come up with your own list of priorities. Know what you like, and get to know any place you're considering.

One way to figure out where to live is to return to places you've enjoyed in the past or to take vacations in locations where you might enjoy retiring. If warmer weather is your goal, visit multiple locations in the area you are considering. If you want to stay in your current community, consider downsizing (see chapter 8) to free up cash. In some markets, downsizing turns into financial upsizing.

Renting First

Unless you know a place very well—you've spent vacations there, for example—you may not want to buy immediately in the new location. Some people do and are quite happy. Look back on your life, and think about times you have relocated—if you have—and what it was like. Certainly moving for work is different than moving in retirement, yet it's worth considering how you made the decisions and which moves went well and why.

During an earlier part of my life, I moved for work twice. The first time, it was from suburban New York to Houston, Texas. The second time, it was from Houston to Alexandria, Virginia, in the greater Washington, D.C., area.

For the first move, I opted to rent first, as I didn't intend to stay in Houston.

When I moved to the Washington area, I found an appealing waterfront building in the City of Alexandria (population 165,300, as of this writing). I knew what I wanted: to be close to Washington without living in it and to be able to drive in a reverse-type commute to my new job a few miles away in Springfield, Virginia.

Researching the building within the first month I arrived, I learned, as a first-time home buyer, I could buy there for almost the same monthly rent. I was meticulous in my research and able to buy for $2,500 down. Okay, so those days are long gone. Yet the point is that sometimes it's better to rent and sometimes it's advantageous to buy.

Each situation is different, and individual finances vary, so consider yours carefully. To ensure your move is the right one, evaluate your current and future finances. One couple from suburban Maryland, prepared for retirement by purchasing a home in Asheville, North Carolina, where they had vacationed. Step by step they are planning to relocate there when he retires from his federal job. At this point, she spends a week each month in Asheville as a transition to the move.

Another couple who had lived in Oregon while raising their children but had relocated to suburban New York for work later in life decided to pull up stakes in advance of retiring and move to their vacation home along the Oregon coast. They traded their New York life for a less expensive one.

Others who choose to move to active-adult communities buy as soon as they find a community they like. In such cases, renting for an extended period of time is typically not an option.

Calculate the Cost

Whatever income you have now will change and typically be smaller in retirement. As described in chapter 2, evaluate your resources. Review these numbers as you calculate the cost of relocating.

Naturally, if you decide to relocate, the expense of transporting your possessions will add to your cost, but it is a one-time expense. For example, if you downsize, you'll have to decide what to keep and what to donate, sell, toss, or store. Will the furnishings you keep and pay to transport fit in the new space? Or will you end up having to replace some items because they don't fit your new lifestyle or space? Measure the new space and your furnishings carefully to help you decide what to bring. Avoid paying to store items that you may never want to use again.

Evaluate the cost and the future cost of any place you are considering.

"I've been planning for retirement for a long time," at least six years, says Rob, 71, who left Half Moon Bay, California, with his wife, Suzanne, after 20 years of living 28 miles south of San Francisco, to live in an active-adult community, Trilogy at Lake Frederick, 90 minutes' drive from Washington, D.C.

Proximity to three airports—Reagan National, Dulles International, and Baltimore-Washington International—appealed to Rob. "Ask yourself where it is you want to live. Your life is going to be different. I don't have to go to work anymore. That's a big change. What is it that you want to do, and where do you want to do it? We wanted to travel."[4] Rob and Suzanne take one or two trips a year overseas and visit family in Massachusetts as well as enjoy day trips in the area.

A key financial step in advance of retiring for Rob, who worked in financial management, and Suzanne, a retired registered nurse, was paying off their mortgage on the California house. "I don't have any mortgage on anything," he says. Nor does he have a car payment. Their homeowner's association fee at Lake Frederick is $325 a month and includes maintenance, such as lawn care. They bought their new house outright but have to pay real estate taxes.

"We can live on Social Security," Rob says, though he has various pensions from different positions throughout his career.[5]

Finding the Right Space

To narrow down what is right for you, ask yourself,

- What kind of space do you prefer? Many prefer to live on one level when they relocate in retirement.
- How much space will you need? Do you anticipate entertaining family and friends in your new location, or do you want a small space that is easy to maintain so you can travel frequently?
- Do you want to maintain the space and property yourself, or will you hire people to help you? Or do you prefer to move to a community where a monthly fee covers maintenance of the property, such as lawn care?
- Do you prefer new construction or an older home?
- Are you looking for a townhouse with an elevator?
- If family members live in the area, can you afford a place nearby? Or do you want to relocate someplace to start a new chapter?

One Colorado couple, both married for the second time, chose to move to an active-adult community in Arizona to start a new life but not be too far from Colorado, where her grown daughter, grandchild, and aging parents still live.

Another couple left Ashburn, Virginia, 35 miles northwest of Washington, D.C., after 10 years to return to San Antonio, Texas, where two of their grown children and grandchildren now live. They traded their three-bedroom, three-level townhouse for a two-bedroom, one-level single-family home. Their housing cost is similar, but the cost of living is considerably lower in their new city. Since they'd lived in San Antonio previously, they knew the area, made a trip to look at property, and bought quickly after looking at many single-family homes in a short period of time. The whole process was quite nerve-racking because of the moving parts and long distance.

Sometimes, even in expensive real estate markets it can be possible to sell a long-term home and find a less expensive place to live. Yet it can take considerable effort. For example, Howard and Paige were quickly able to sell their five-bedroom house in McLean, Virginia. Yet finding the right place to live in the area required research and time. Like other empty nesters, they found preparing to move from a large space to a much smaller one was part of the challenge.

"We want to be near our grandchildren and our children," says Howard, a retired engineer. All three of their grown children expected to move to the Washington, D.C., area, and two already had. So the couple began looking at high-rise condominiums in nearby downtown Bethesda, Maryland, and at condominiums and townhouses throughout the area. "We didn't want the steps," Paige says. Much of what they saw cost more than they wanted to spend for less space than they needed—one-bedroom condominiums for $600,000 to $800,000. While driving around the area they found an older condominium development dating to the 1970s on 28 wooded acres. Within a few minutes' walk to a suburban shopping center, the development has tennis courts, adult and children's swimming pools, and a community center, as well as a gatehouse that controls access by vehicle.

Ultimately, they traded 3,300 square feet for 1,200 square feet when they purchased a two-bedroom unit with a patio and private garden in the condominium development. "I gave away so many memories and memorabilia," Paige says. They gave some of their art to their children but discarded items they didn't want. "It's heartbreaking, but you do it because this really is the best step." Howard had to consolidate a library full of books for the move.

A major advantage of the move was the freedom to travel without worrying about the five-bedroom home they sold. With the condominium, they can have the community security staff check on their unit if they are going to be away for an extended period of time. "We can pick up and go," she says.

In addition, the price was right. At the time, two-bedroom units were selling for just under $500,000.[6]

Sharing Space

For some people, finding a new location and sharing space can be the answer.

Yet where to live and with whom can be the dilemma. Marianne Kilkenny was in her mid-50s when she decided to stop living and working in Silicon Valley. At first, she was not sure what to do next. While reading Joan Medlicott's novel The Ladies of Covington Send Their Love during a visit to Asheville, North Carolina, she was inspired. A year later, Kilkenny, now 70, moved to Asheville with a plan to create communities like the fictional one she'd read about: three women in their 60s living together in a farmhouse in North Carolina.[7]

Indeed, the 1980s and '90s television show The Golden Girls depicted a similar situation, where four previously married women lived together in Miami.

Housing typically consumes a third or more of living expenses for people age 55 and older, driving the desire to share living space. Yet another reason can be the wish for companionship or the sense of security a housemate or housemates can provide in times when family members are living far apart.[8]

Carrying Debt

Certainly carrying debt into retirement will limit your dreams. Mortgage debt, vehicle debt, and credit card debt are the three most likely forms. More homeowners 65 and older are still making mortgage payments, according to a May 2014 Consumer Financial Protection Bureau report.[9] In fact, 30 percent of those homeowners are carrying a mortgage, up from 22 percent a decade earlier. Among those 75 and older, the percentage carrying a mortgage nearly tripled to 21.2 percent, up from 8.4 percent, during the same period.

Carrying a mortgage can limit your options as you approach retirement, but it's not possible for everyone to pay it off before they retire. For example, if you relocated during your working life to a more expensive market, sold your previous property, and bought one in the new location, you may have been propelled into mortgage debt that you might not otherwise have had in your 50s or 60s. Or perhaps you bought a home later in life—say, in your 40s—and therefore are still carrying a mortgage.

Some believe, at least while they are still working, it is better to carry a mortgage, especially one at a low interest rate, like 3 to 4 percent. They reason they can be earning 5 to 6 percent or more on their investments rather than paying down or paying off the mortgage. That can be advantageous while they continue to work and need a tax deduction. Yet if you approach retirement and no longer need a tax deduction on your income, and you have adequate resources, it may be better to pay off the mortgage.

Once you have retired and given up your paycheck, another option is to sell the property, pay off the remaining mortgage, and find a less expensive property in the same or different location in a milder climate.

Sometimes a family home can be your dream location, living on land that has been in your family for generations. That was the case for one couple who sold their house in Queens, New York, for $780,000 in 2013. Having paid off their mortgage in 2008, they were able to earmark less than half of the money to buy out the family home in New England from his sibling.[10]

Yet one of the lessons learned since retiring almost eight years ago was a tendency to underestimate living expenses in retirement. "We just didn't think of everything," he says. "Nor did we realize that some of the things we thought of would be as expensive as they turned out to be"—45 to 50 percent more, he says. Despite all their planning and discussions with financial experts, health insurance costs until they were eligible for Medicare and a

30 percent increase in property taxes over five years were among the largest unanticipated expenses. Other costs he hadn't taken into account included vehicle and home maintenance and repairs. "When we were doing our planning, a new roof never came into the discussion," he says. A cost that might not seem significant when you are still working can become magnified once you have retired. In addition, their kitchen needed work.[11]

Yet the silver lining for him is living on land that has been in his family for generations. In addition, he intended to wait until 65 to claim Social Security.[12]

Sadly, his wife has since passed away.

Each year, numerous websites create lists of the best (and worst) places to retire based on criteria such as affordability, popularity on the site, access to medical care, crime, weather, and culture. What about transportation? Access to airports?

While lists can be fun or interesting to read, keep in mind, as we said above, that where and how you retire is a very personal decision. Make sure your choice suits you: your budget, your needs, your preferences.

Ask yourself, what will it actually cost to live in a certain place? Research the cost of each location you are considering to the extent possible. For example, if there will be monthly condominium fees, determine how much they might increase each year. Even without monthly fees, housing requires maintenance. Add that to your expenses.

If you aren't aiming to relocate near family, this can mean more flexibility in choosing a place to live in retirement. Or it can mean more resources to live in one or more places.

No State Income Tax

There are some people who simply don't want to live in a state that has state income tax. If you live in one of these states, you won't have to pay taxes on your wages or income from Social Security, pensions, or retirement plans, such as 401(k)s or IRAs. Yet taxpayers are subject to other types of taxes, including local taxes or sales tax. The following are the states that do not have state income tax:

- Alaska
- Florida
- Nevada
- South Dakota

- Texas
- Washington
- Wyoming[13]

Two more states with no state income tax do tax dividends and interest income, but they expect to phase out that tax in future years so that they'll be tax free by 2025:

- New Hampshire
- Tennessee[14]

Further, the majority of states—37—do not tax Social Security retirement benefits, but thirteen do:

- Colorado
- Connecticut
- Kansas
- Minnesota
- Missouri
- Montana
- Nebraska
- New Mexico
- Rhode Island
- Utah
- Vermont
- West Virginia

Yet you may have to pay federal income tax on part of those Social Security retirement benefits.[15] Approximately 40 percent of people who receive Social Security have to pay income taxes on their benefits.[16]

Generally, if your total annual income is less than $25,000, you won't have to pay tax on your Social Security retirement benefits. At the end of each year, the Social Security Administration will mail you a Social Security Benefit Statement (Form SSA-1099), which shows the amount of benefits you have received during the year. Use it when you are completing your federal income tax return to determine if you owe taxes on the benefits, or give it to your accountant or tax preparer. You are not required to have the SSA withhold federal taxes, but you may prefer to have taxes withheld. Refer to the IRS's *Tax Guide for Seniors* for help with paying tax on Social Security benefits.[17]

Figuring out where to live in retirement takes planning and research. Some people know they will move to their second home full-time in retirement, while others plan to relocate to a city where one or more of their children and grandchildren live. Others move in with family members in a separate suite within the house. Whatever you decide to do, consider the cost and comfort of your decision.

Read on to learn how important transportation will be in retirement, especially if you can no longer drive.

~

CHAPTER ELEVEN

How You'll Get Around
In Case You Can't Drive

When making plans to retire, transportation is often an afterthought. Yet weaving transportation into plans is essential.[1] Typically those who are still driving believe they always will.

"When people make retirement plans, they make no transportation plans because they assume they're going to drive forever," says Katherine Freund, founder and president of the Independent Transportation Network of America (ITNAmerica), a nonprofit organization that provides rides for older adults.[2]

Outliving Driving

In fact, according findings published in the *American Journal of Public Health*, Americans outlive their ability to drive safely—for women by 10 years on average, and for men by seven years.[3]

Most people view driving a vehicle as freedom, especially those who came of age in the 1960s. Yet there is a small but growing interest in a car-free life, which has developed among millennials and older people in places such as Arlington, Virginia, a county just outside of Washington, D.C., that has won awards from the American Planning Association for smart growth.

Still, in the United States the ability to get around without a vehicle mostly has been limited to large urban centers such as New York City, particularly Manhattan, where mass transit, including subways and buses, has developed an extensive transportation network used by people of all socioeconomic backgrounds throughout the tiny island—13.4 miles long and 2.3 miles wide at its widest point.

In Manhattan, an area of 22.7 square miles, walking, buses, subways, taxis, pedicabs, and ride-hailing companies as well as private vehicles are among the ways to get from one place to another. Once you leave the city limits— the other boroughs and beyond—owning a vehicle becomes more common and necessary.

Yet in the United States three-quarters of those 65 and older live in rural or suburban communities, where getting from place to place depends on private vehicles. Older adults in the United States take nine out of ten personal trips by car, either as drivers or passengers. In an aging population, vehicle dependence creates safety and transportation problems for older drivers. Those who drive face the "highest crash risk per mile of any group except teenagers." If they stop driving, their transportation options are limited.[4]

Less Driving

Deciding not to drive is different from realizing you are no longer fit to drive. It typically happens incrementally. You might decide to stop driving to unfamiliar places at night. Whatever the reason, depending on the available transportation options where you live, not driving can limit your autonomy.[5]

So when figuring out where to live in retirement, be sure to consider your transportation options. Some people drive until the end of their lives. If they've always lived a suburban or rural lifestyle that has always required driving, that's all they know.

Yet vision problems and mobility and cognitive issues can limit vehicle use or stop it entirely.

Where You Live

Transportation needs depend on where you live and where you might want to live when you retire. Yet, your health is the single biggest factor that determines whether you're able to drive safely as you age. Some people can drive into their 80s and 90s, while others start to cut back at 65 or earlier. Recent findings from the AAA LongRoad (Longitudinal Research on Aging Drivers) Study, a multiyear research program that aims to better understand and meet the safety and mobility of older drivers in the United States, shows that one in five older drivers reduced their driving in the prior year. Of the study's 2,990 participants, more women (57 percent) than men (43 percent) reported driving less.[6]

The Impact of Not Driving

According to research funded by the Centers for Disease Control and Prevention, by 2025 approximately 20 percent of drivers will be age 65 or older. If they are unable to drive or find alternate transportation, they risk becoming isolated. More than half of these nondrivers stay home in part because they don't have transportation. Nondrivers also make 15 percent fewer trips to the doctor than older drivers and 65 percent fewer trips for social, family, and religious activities.[7]

The inability to drive can be temporary or can gradually become permanent. Not driving can limit your social life, depending on where you live.[8]

Losing autonomy in itself creates problems for older people. "The loss of independence—the sudden inability to drive a car—causes them incredible distress" in addition to affecting their mobility, says retired lawyer John Lemega, a volunteer driver with ITNAmerica Central Connecticut. For-profit transportation like taxis and ride shares can add up quickly, and "a lot of people we deal with don't have that kind of income."[9]

Driving Others

Ever since the invention of automobiles, people have been driving other people. Providing rides through a third party dates back to 1961 through the Friends in Service Helping (FISH) program that began in England. The first FISH chapter in the United States organized in 1964 in West Springfield, Massachusetts. FISH chapters throughout the United States offer, among other services, free rides for medical transportation for those in need.[10]

In areas where public transportation is limited or almost nonexistent, finding nonprofit and for-profit organizations that provide rides can be the solution for people who don't have family in the area or find they need more options to get around.

Those who don't use smartphones or apps can contact https://gogogrand parent.com/. For nonprofit services in your area, search https://www.ridesin sight.org/ or https://ctaa.org/national-volunteer-transportation-center/.

For those who are unable to use fixed-route buses, paratransit can be an option. Typically it is available for people who have a disability and requires a doctor's note. Another option is to live in a community that has an established virtual "village," a group of volunteers that help each other and often offers rides to older people. Visit the Village to Village Network, https://www.vtvnetwork.org/, to determine if your community or one to which you are considering a move has a virtual village.

Even in cities like Washington, D.C., with strong public transportation systems that extend into suburban neighborhoods, it's often the last mile that is the hardest for older people. Getting from public transportation to your final destination or walking a mile or more to a bus stop might not be possible, especially in winter snow and ice or summer heat and humidity. Even getting on and off a bus can be an obstacle for some.[11]

Planning Ahead

When planning where you are going to live in retirement, Lemega says, "have transportation be among the major factors you consider." For example, in the West Hartford area, he says, mass transit is "will-o'-the-wisp—it's not real." There is a bus to downtown Hartford from outlying areas, but "most people don't really know how to ride the buses and are fearful of asking the question, How do I do this?"[12]

Travel planning can start even if you are driving. "If you're 55, you have to project out into the future," says gerontologist Judi Bonilla, who founded We Get Around, a nonprofit that promotes the use of public transportation for adults.[13] Author of *Freewheeling after Sixty: Your Guide to Freedom and Mobility*, Bonilla teaches small groups of seniors how to use public transportation in San Diego. "With age comes experience and quite possibly medical conditions that may affect your driving," she writes. "Chronic conditions include arthritis, diabetes, macular degeneration, multiple sclerosis, Parkinson's disease, seizures, and sleep disorders. Having a medical condition does not automatically disqualify you from driving. However, it's important for your safety and that of others that you diligently manage and monitor your condition."[14]

Travel Training

Though not everyone can learn how to use public transportation, riding trolleys, subways, and buses can open up a whole world to those who are able to use them. The sooner you learn how, the more likely you are to be mobile longer.

Consider Maria who used to drive 18 miles to get downtown from Lakeside, California, in the eastern part of San Diego County. Now she drives to a nearby Metropolitan Transit System Trolley stop where she parks her car for free and rides about an hour to performances at Spreckels Theatre, the San Diego Civic Theatre, and the Lyceum and Balboa theaters. "I like musicals," she says. "If it's a musical, I'm in." She used to drive straight to the venues.

Yet, when she found competing for a parking space was becoming too stressful for her, she added public transportation to her route. "I was glad I could find a different way to get there," she says.[15]

A few years ago Maria, now 79, enrolled in a travel-training class with We Get Around. It changed her life. A former dancer who lived in New York City before moving to California with her late husband, Maria typically goes to the theater on weekends. "It's something to look forward to and not feel so confined," she says. "You got to get out and about. Whenever I get on the trolley, I say, 'Thank G–d for Judi [Bonilla].' It's not like New York where you just get on the subway. We don't have that here."[16]

In areas where driving is king, older adults are likely to depend on family members and friends for rides. Unfortunately, younger family members and friends won't always be able to drive those in their 80s and 90s, especially when they have relocated to warmer climates, away from family.[17]

Without a support system, retirees may drive beyond the time when it is safe for them to be behind the wheel, according to Bonilla.[18]

Analyze Your Situation

Evaluate your current neighborhood in terms of where you typically need and want to go, and determine how you might reach those places if you were no longer driving. Which five places are most important? Supermarket? Pharmacy? Children's home? Doctor's office? Place of worship? Include leisure activities like classes, entertainment, and simply meeting friends. "Think about how you're going to do that when you can no longer drive," says Bonilla. "Lay out a grid and see how far these trips are from your home. That will determine where you live, whether you stay in your home."[19] Do you have relatives or friends who would have the time to help you? What is the public transportation like? Can you afford to take taxis or use ride-hailing services, if they exist where you live? Is there a volunteer transportation network in your community?

Preparing

The time to prepare for when you cut back or can no longer drive is long before that day arrives.

Here are some steps to take:

- If you are considering relocation, "be sure that there is some kind of transportation network in the community that provides door-to-door services," Katherine   Freund says. In order to use the Independent Transportation Network, riders fund a personal transportation account in advance. All riders receive a monthly statement that details every payment. Charges are often lower than taxi fees, Freund says. Drivers are required to assist riders with packages. No tipping is allowed.[20]

- Evaluate what your needs will be over time. Consider the activities you love and the services you will need. What are your hobbies? Are there any groups you might enjoy and want to join? How will you get there?

- If possible, before relocating, live in any new community you are considering for three months or longer, especially if it's a seasonal place, Bonilla says.[21]

- If you plan to keep driving, check with AAA to ensure your car fits you ergonomically and to learn about renewing your driver's license in your new location.

- To improve your driving, consider a refresher course from AARP or AAA, at https://seniordriving.aaa.com/ and https://www.aarpdriver safety.org/.

- Inquire if any senior-housing communities you are considering have shuttle buses that provide transportation for shopping, religious services, and doctor visits.[22]

- Rather than thinking of giving up driving as a loss, spend time and energy researching other options. "It's not giving up your independence; it's doing something in a different way," Bonilla says. "It's alternatives. People have fear of alternatives and the unknown," such as using public transportation.[23]

Walkability

Walkability is an increasingly important factor in choosing a place to live, especially where mixed-use development has been on the rise. This type of development combines residential living spaces with retail, for example, enabling residents to walk to some, if not many, services. If and when you decide to relocate, determine in advance how many places you can reach on foot by searching https://www.walkscore.com/. The higher the walk score, the more services and amenities will be reachable on foot. Staying fit and healthy is essential to being able to walk to nearby services, and walking won't work for everyone. Building and maintaining your endurance, strength, flexibility, and balance improve your chances. Increasingly, older people are using pedal-assist bicycles and three-wheelers.

Even if you are in your 50s, it's a good time to think ahead to a time when you might be unable to drive. If you are in your 60s, research the options available in your community or another place to which you might move. If you are considering an active-adult community, inquire whether it has a shuttle and where and when it can accommodate your needs. It's better to know what's available than be isolated later in life.

If you plan to travel outside your immediate area, read on for tips for planning your best trips yet.

CHAPTER TWELVE

~

Exploring the World

Deciding Where to Go and How to Pay for It

If you are like many baby boomers, you enjoy spending time with family, adventure, exploration, and learning new things. One of the most popular ways of experiencing all four is through travel.

Baby boomers were expected to spend, on average, $7,800, in 2020, up from $6,600 a year earlier, according to an AARP report. They were planning to travel to more expensive destinations, spend more time in those places, stay in higher quality accommodations, and participate in more activities.[1]

What is driving baby boomer travel? Research shows that about 59 percent wish to spend time with family and friends, 51 percent seek to escape their everyday lives, and 45 percent aim to relax and rejuvenate. Approximately one in four baby boomers planning international travel cites a "bucket list" trip; 12 percent anticipate taking multigenerational trips, and another 12 percent plan to embark on "solo travel." Of those who planned a domestic trip for 2020, 15 percent were multigenerational.[2]

Yet a lot changed with COVID-19. Many people began rethinking whether, where, and how to travel. In addition, they encountered various travel restrictions across the country and globe. With three vaccines available as of this writing, more of those who love to travel have begun booking air flights, hotels, cruises, and trains. As the world becomes safer, many more still hope to travel. Anticipate changes. For example, airlines may decide to verify your COVID-19 test results and vaccine status.[3]

Planning Your Trips

Whether you've traveled before or have postponed traveling until your retirement years, figuring out how to pay for travel is crucial. Planning is essential for getting the most for your money.

Besides traditional travel such as prearranged tours, hiring a car and driver, or joining an alumnae club tour, there are ways to travel for less, including home exchanges, home rentals, buying mobile homes or recreational vehicles, and volunteering.

If you're already retired or are 10 or fewer years from your projected retirement date, begin to prioritize the places you want to visit and how much money you will allocate to travel during a particular year. "Decide where you want to spend your money," says Anne Scully, president of McCabe World Travel in McLean, Virginia. "What's the hardest trip? Do it first." In addition, before you travel, estimate the cost of the trip. "Look at the final price," Scully says, including all your costs once you leave your hotel or ship. Selecting all-inclusive trips and cruises can help when calculating the final cost of a trip before you travel.[4] When you purchase air and hotel in a bundle through an online travel agency, you can save up to 40 percent.[5]

Spending

Regardless of how much money they have, most people think about how much money they want to spend, even at the highest levels. "Everybody has a budget," says Bowden Sarrett, travel adviser at Brownell Travel in Mobile, Alabama, a member of the Virtuoso network of travel agencies. "Everybody's got their limits."[6]

If travel is a priority for you in retirement, planning ahead can not only make it possible but also help it proceed smoothly. How much you've traveled already in your life can determine where you want to go and the type of trips you prefer. Typically, the more you've already traveled, the more selective you are likely to be.

Volunteering

For Marie and John, for example, assisting scientific researchers on an Earthwatch Institute trip to Tuscany was not only exhilarating and educational, it was also tax-deductible. They spent seven days at what had once been an Etruscan fort, helping an archaeologist excavate the site in the seaside city of Populonia. The trip cost them $1,600 each, plus airfare. They stayed in a three-bedroom apartment in a gated community, sharing a bathroom with another couple. At the time, Marie had recently retired as a teacher and John was still working.[7]

The couple had traveled through their working years rather than wait until they retired. They had saved for travel in a separate vacation club account through a credit union while she had still been teaching.[8]

When their Earthwatch trip ended, they spent four days in Florence, where they had booked a small, relatively inexpensive hotel, and walked everywhere.[9]

Others volunteer through the federal government, such as for the National Park Service, for the Bureau of Land Management, at Forest Service sites, or through the Army Corps of Engineers.[10]

For example, a few years ago Grand Portage National Monument offered the opportunity to be a living history volunteer, interpreting North American fur trade history and Ojibwe culture in three eight-hour shifts a week. When they weren't dressed in period costumes typical of the year 1797, participants had time to hike, canoe, and kayak in and near Lake Superior in northeastern Minnesota.[11]

Check the portal at https://www.volunteer.gov/s/ to find opportunities near you or farther away.

Getting Paid to Travel

If volunteering is not your style, you may be able to find some work that includes travel and pays. Some retired people find jobs aboard cruise ships. For example, MSC Cruises has hired retired and semiretired people as guest lecturers, port lecturers, language teachers, and arts and crafts instructors.[12] Mary, who had worked in sales for 34 years and postponed traveling, developed an interest in wine, which led her to take courses, which in turn led to working at a vineyard in the tasting room, and then to working on a cruise ship as a wine educator. She'd made a connection while working in the tasting room that opened up the cruise ship job. A complimentary cabin and food made up for the relatively minimal pay.[13]

Regular Saving

Others make saving for travel a goal and spend accordingly on a regular basis. One single mother in her early 60s describes a simple way to prioritize spending: Rather than getting that extra latte, saving for a trip wins out for her. Her trip list is long, so even small sacrifices make a difference.

Cruises

If you prefer cruises to land trips, be aware that the cost of a cruise varies depending on the level of cruise line you choose, the type of ship, and the destination. At this writing, cruise travel has begun to open up in parts of the world. US guidelines are still pending.

"Cruise pricing is really variable," says Colleen Daniel, editor-in-chief of CruiseCritic.com, a consumer cruise website. "Prices can change multiple times a day." A guide for cost is to think in terms of paying $100 per person, per night, she says. Luxury ships can cost as much as $500 to $1,000 per person, per night, while mass-market ships typically cost $150 to $200 per person, per night for an inside cabin, usually without a window or balcony. Cruise pricing is not all-inclusive, as shore excursions, alcoholic beverages, and some dining options are extra.[14] River cruises are another option, and prices vary depending on class of ship and destination. Airfare to the cruise port of embarkation is typically additional. When evaluating a cruise price, whether on a cruise line or online travel agency website or through a brick-and-mortar travel agency, ask if the price cited includes port charges and taxes.

Air Travel

For far-flung land trips as well as those in the United States, set up airfare alerts with an airline for which you have miles or points, or use airfarewatch dog.com.

Here are other ways to save on transportation:

- Consider an alternate airport, if the fare is lower, or a flight with one or more stops, or choose a discount airline. Nonstop flights are typically more expensive.
- Book each passenger in a group on a separate reservation in case there is one lower fare still available. Passengers on the same reservation must book all tickets at the same price. If there is one lower-priced seat available, you can save a bit.
- For US rail, travel on Amtrak, where booking at least seven to 14 days in advance for many routes can save you 20 percent on regular adult fares. Check for updates at https://www.amtrak.com.
- If you are traveling in a group of up to four passengers on Amtrak, you can save up to 35 percent. Savings are available on long-distance trains and connecting buses as well as Amtrak Northeast Regional trains for coach seats only.

- If you are 65 or older, take advantage of a 10 percent discount on most rail fares on most Amtrak trains.
- Ride Megabus between US towns and cities for as little as $1. If you want to travel but don't have a specific destination in mind, check https://us.megabus.com/fare-finder for destinations and fare deals.[15]

Accommodations

If you have options about where and when you travel, you can find affordable accommodations. "If you can be flexible on the date of arrival and which hotel, you can get a lower rate," says Bjorn Hanson, a New York–based hospitality consultant. "Instead of arriving on a Friday, arrive on a Sunday" to get a better rate, he advises. To avoid higher weekend rates typically charged at leisure hotels and resorts, arrive Wednesday instead of Friday. If you prefer a certain hotel brand, try a less expensive tier within that brand. For example, instead of staying at a Marriott or JW Marriott, check the price at a Courtyard Marriott or a Residence Inn.[16]

Another way to save is to exchange your home for a stay in someone else's home.

Sites to check are homeaway.com, myplaceforyours.com, homeexchange.com, or homeforexchange.com. One couple in their mid-60s from Washington state began using home exchanges in 2013. "No money exchanges hands," she says. "They're going to take care of my house like I'm going to take care of yours."[17]

Yet everyone won't be comfortable with exchange arrangements. "The scary part, of course, is opening your home to total strangers," writes Glenn Ruffenach in the *Wall Street Journal.* Home exchanges do involve risks, and cancellations are among the most common. Be prepared for the other party to back out of the swap.[18]

"You will need to vet—as thoroughly as possible—the people who are moving into your home. References are a must, and home-exchange websites can tell you how many previous swaps, if any, your would-be visitors have had." Exchange partners might damage your home, possessions, or vehicle. Ask your insurance carrier if adding riders to your home and vehicle insurance to cover temporary occupants will protect you.[19]

Here are other ways to save on accommodations:

- Telephone the hotel's front desk and ask for the lowest rate available.
- Are any senior rates available, and is that rate lower than any current special?

- Choose accommodations that include free breakfast, or ask for a refrigerator for your room. Or book accommodations with a kitchen so you can prepare some meals rather than always eating in restaurants.
- Determine if the hotel charges a "resort" fee, a daily per-person charge that is added to the price of a room at some hotels but often not included in the listed price for the room. Ask what it includes. You might be able to negotiate breakfast rather than laundry or other services you don't need.
- Find free nights by checking deals on a hotel or online travel agency website. Special offers can include deals where you book five nights and get two nights free or book three nights and get one night free.
- Ask for transfers before you leave home. Check with your hotel or travel agent if the hotel or resort offers a free shuttle between the airport and the hotel. You'll avoid tacking costs onto your trip by paying for taxis or ride shares.[20]
- Become a rewards member for one or more hotel groups, and stay at their properties as often as possible. In addition, get a branded credit card with the same hotel group to obtain points on all spending. With enough points, you may gain access to hotel clubs with complimentary food.
- "Protect yourself and your travel investment," says Anne Scully. Will your health insurance cover you while traveling? Medicare generally doesn't pay for health care or supplies received outside the United States. There are exceptions. Visit https://www.medicare.gov/coverage /travel. But Medigap—Medicare supplemental plans—and Medicare Advantage plans often help pay for emergency care overseas. Even with those, it is advisable to buy travel insurance with emergency health coverage and trip-interruption protection in the event of any unforeseen medical concerns.[21]
- Consider renting an apartment for longer stays. Sites such as onefine stay.com help travelers find luxury accommodations with a kitchen and a washer and dryer.
- Use a credit card without foreign transaction fees for purchases made while traveling internationally.
- Extend family visits and trips for celebrations and milestones to give yourself time to explore.[22]
- Watch out for travel scams that offer deals that may be too good to be true, whether they're related to airfares or to vacation packages, hotel rooms, or timeshares. Rely on companies you know are reputable; be wary of any deals offered through pop-up ads online, unsolicited phone

calls, or unfamiliar websites. Search travel companies, hotels, rentals, and agents online using the words "scam," "review," or "complaint."[23]
- File complaints with a local consumer agency such as the Better Business Bureau. "Most federal agencies don't attempt to mediate individual complaints," says Susan Grant, director of consumer protection and privacy at the Consumer Federation of America. Consumers should "contact a local or state consumer protection agency to see if they can help resolve their individual problem or refer them to another agency."[24]

Overload

As appealing as travel is, there can be too much of a good thing. I experienced something similar while living in New York City: Too many operas, too many Broadway shows, too much of what perhaps grows from what has become known as FOMO—the fear of missing out. You may not always be aware of this; I wasn't. It creeps up on you as you find the incessant pleasure-seeking becomes what one New York bachelor called a "merry-go-round."

Geriatric psychiatrist Marc E. Agronin aptly describes this phenomenon among retirees in an article he wrote for the *Wall Street Journal*: "As they travel the world to soak up experiences, too many seniors inevitably lose track of what really matters—their connections to family, friends, and community. They feel like strangers in their own homes. Eventually the bucket list becomes something of an addiction: The high from an adventure doesn't last, so seniors find themselves piling on experiences to keep the thrills coming, further alienating them from real life back home."[25]

Rather than an endless pursuit of pleasure, search for something "much deeper and more meaningful,"[26] whether through travel shared with grandchildren, volunteer activities, or connections with family, friends, and community.

"There's a way out of this trap. Retirees should think about using all of the advantages that make a bucket list possible, such as wealth and vigor, to build something much deeper and more meaningful," Agronin writes.[27]

If you think of the purpose of your travel, why you want to go to a particular place, it can be a different experience. Whatever drives you, take some time to think about it so you can gain or give the most from the travel experiences.

Before planning any travel, it's best to check the US State Department website for travel advisories and warnings, https://travel.state.gov/content/travel.html. Situations worldwide are in flux.

Happy and safe travels!

APPENDIX

~

Retirement Resources

Budgeting

The Vanguard Group's Retirement-Expense Worksheet, https://personal
.vanguard.com/us/insights/retirement/tool/retirement-expense-work
sheet

The Vanguard Group's Retirement-Income Worksheet, https://personal
.vanguard.com/us/insights/retirement/tool/retirement-income-work
sheet

Health

Medicare, https://www.medicare.gov/medicare-you-handbook

Housing

Communities for people 55 years of age and older, https://www.55places
.com/

Continuing-care retirement communities, https://www.caring.com/senior
-living/continuing-care-retirement-communities/

Florida for Boomers, https://www.floridaforboomers.com/

National Shared Housing Resource Center, https://nationalsharedhousing
.org/

ideal-LIVING, https://www.ideal-living.com/

Top Retirements, https://www.topretirements.com/

Jobs

Jobs for people over 50, https://retirementjobs.com/
Career resources for seniors, https://www.workforce50.com/
Professional development, https://getfive.com/
Job-search portal, https://jobs.aarp.org/
Job-search and -training portal sponsored by the US Department of Labor, https://www.onetonline.org

Education

Online courses, certifications, and degree programs, https://www.coursera.org
Postsecondary scholarships to colleges and universities, https://www.osherfoundation.org/
Virtual online classes, https://www.oasisnet.org/

Social Security

The US Social Security Administration, https://www.ssa.gov/

Transportation

AAA, https://seniordriving.aaa.com/
AARP, https://www.aarpdriversafety.org/
Community Transportation Association of America, https://ctaa.org/national-volunteer-transportation-center/
GoGo, https://gogograndparent.com/
Rides in Sight, https://www.ridesinsight.org/
Village to Village Network, https://www.vtvnetwork.org/content.aspx
Walk Score, https://www.walkscore.com/

~

Notes

Chapter One

1. Board of Governors of the Federal Reserve System, *Survey of Consumer Finances, 1989–2019*, Federal Reserve System, last updated September 28, 2020, https://www.federalreserve.gov/econres/scf/dataviz/scf/chart/#series:Retirement_Accounts;demographic:agecl;population:all;units:median.

2. ATTOM staff, "Q3 2019 Foreclosure Activity Down 19 Percent from Year Ago to Lowest Level since Q2 2005," Attom Data Solutions, October 15, 2019, https://www.attomdata.com/news/market-trends/attom-data-solutions-q3-2019-u-s-foreclosure-market-report/.

3. Richard Fry, "The Pace of Boomer Retirements Has Accelerated in the Past Year," Pew Research Center, November 9, 2020, https://www.pewresearch.org/fact-tank/2020/11/09/the-pace-of-boomer-retirements-has-accelerated-in-the-past-year/.

4. "Frequently Requested Data: Workers with Pension Coverage by Type of Plan, 1983, 1998, and 2016," Center for Retirement Research at Boston College, last updated February 2018, http://crr.bc.edu/wp-content/uploads/2015/10/figure-16.pdf.

5. Richard Fry, "Americans Are Moving at Historically Low Rates, in Part Because Millennials Are Staying Put," Fact Tank, Pew Research Center, February 13, 2017, https://www.pewresearch.org/fact-tank/2017/02/13/americans-are-moving-at-historically-low-rates-in-part-because-millennials-are-staying-put/.

6. "CFPB Spotlights Mortgage Debt Challenges Faced by Older Americans," Newsroom, Consumer Financial Protection Bureau, May 7, 2014, https://www.consumerfinance.gov/about-us/newsroom/cfpb-spotlights-mortgage-debt-challenges-faced-by-older-americans/.

7. Harriet Edleson, "Selling the Family Home Is Liberating for Many Retirees," *New York Times*, October 19, 2014, https://www.nytimes.com/2014/12/20/your-money/selling-the-family-home-is-liberating-for-many-retirees.html.

8. Ibid.

9. Lydia Saad, "What Percentage of Americans Owns Stock?" The Short Answer, Gallup, September 13, 2019, https://news.gallup.com/poll/266807/percentage-americans-owns-stock.aspx.

10. Calculated via the longevity calculator at ssa.gov: "Retirement and Survivor's Benefits: Life Expectancy Calculator," Social Security Administration, accessed December 16, 2020, https://www.ssa.gov/OACT/population/longevity.html.

11. Harriet Edleson, "Almost Half of Americans Fear Running Out of Money in Retirement," AARP.org, May 21, 2019, https://www.aarp.org/retirement/planning-for-retirement/info-2019/retirees-fear-losing-money.html.

12. Society of Actuaries Committee on Post Retirement Needs and Risks, Urban Institute, and Women's Institute for a Secure Retirement, "The Impact of Running Out of Money in Retirement," November 2012, https://www.wiserwomen.org/wp-content/uploads/2018/01/Impact-running-out-of-money-retirement-report-2012.pdf.

13. Michael D. Hurd and Susann Rohwedder, "Economic Preparation for Retirement," NBER working paper #17203, July 8 (Cambridge, MA: National Bureau of Economic Research, 2011), https://www.nber.org/system/files/working_papers/w17203/w17203.pdf.

14. Ibid.

15. Harriet Edleson, "Taking a Job Out of the Financial Equation," *New York Times*, April 18, 2014, https://www.nytimes.com/2014/04/19/your-money/taking-a-job-out-of-the-financial-equation.html.

16. Catherine Collinson, Patti Rowey, and Heidi Cho, *What Is "Retirement"? Three Generations Prepare for Older Age: 19th Annual Transamerica Retirement Survey of Workers*, Transamerica Center for Retirement Studies report, April (Los Angeles: Transamerica Institute, 2019), https://transamericacenter.org/docs/default-source/retirement-survey-of-workers/tcrs2019_sr_what_is_retirement_by_generation.pdf.

17. Edleson, "Taking a Job."

18. Ibid.

19. Mark Hinkle, "Social Security Announces 1.3 Percent Benefit Increase for 2021," press release, Social Security Administration, October 13, 2020, https://www.ssa.gov/news/press/releases/2020/#10-2020-1.

20. Edleson, "Taking a Job."

21. George Kinder, *Life Planning for You: How to Design and Deliver the Life of Your Dreams*, with Mary Rowland ([Littleton, MA]: Serenity Point Press, 2014).

22. Society of Actuaries, "Deciding When to Claim Social Security," Managing Retirement Decisions Series, 2017, https://www.soa.org/globalassets/assets/Files/Research/research-pen-deciding-ss.pdf.

23. "When to Start Receiving Retirement Benefits," pub. no. 05-10147, Social Security Administration, January 2021, https://www.ssa.gov/pubs/EN-05-10147.pdf.

24. Ibid.

25. Author's e-mail exchange with public affairs personnel at the Social Security Administration, 2019.

26. You can find the Vanguard Group's worksheet by visiting https://personal .vanguard.com/us/insights/retirement/tool/retirement-expense-worksheet.

Chapter Two

1. Board of Governors of the Federal Reserve System, *Survey of Consumer Finances, 1989–2019*.

2. Harriet Edleson, "How to Budget for Retirement: Running the Numbers Is Key if You're within Five Years of Retirement," *Next Avenue*, August 16, 2016, https://www.nextavenue.org/how-to-budget-for-retirement/.

3. See the Social Security Administration's Life Expectancy Calculator at https://www.ssa.gov/oact/population/longevity.html.

4. Calculated at ibid.

5. Catherine Collinson, *Retirement through the Ages: Expectations and Preparations of American Workers*, Transamerica Center for Retirement Studies report (Los Angeles: Transamerica Institute, May 2015), https://www.transamericacenter.org /docs/default-source/resources/center-research/16th-annual/tcrs2015_sr_retirement _throughout_the_ages.pdf.

6. "The Pandemic's Impact on Workers' Finances Has Long-Term Repercussions for Retirement Security," press release, Transamerica Center for Retirement, December 18, 2020, https://transamericacenter.org/docs/default-source/retirement-survey-of -workers/tcrs2020_pr_20th_annual_worker_compendium_press_release.pdf. Find the actual report at Catherine Collinson, Patti Vogt Rowey, and Heidi Cho, *Retirement Security: A Compendium of Findings about US Workers; 20th Annual Transamerica Retirement Survey of Workers*, Transamerica Center for Retirement, December 2020, https://transamericacenter.org/docs/default-source/retirement-survey-of-workers /tcrs2020_sr_20th_annual_compendium_of_workers_report.pdf. And also see Harriet Edleson, "Retirement Savings Shortfall? Get a Part-Time Job: Finding the Right Type of Work Might Require Some Type of Creativity," *Next Avenue*, August 18, 2015, https://www.nextavenue.org/retirement-savings-shortfall-get-a-part-time-job/.

7. Edleson, "Taking a Job."

8. "Snapshot of Older Consumers and Mortgage Debt," Office for Older Americans, Consumer Financial Protection Bureau, May 2014, https://files.consumerfinance .gov/f/201405_cfpb_snapshot_older-consumers-mortgage-debt.pdf. And see Edleson, "Selling the Family Home."

9. Author phone interview with Lauren Zangardi Haynes, January 11, 2018.

10. Author phone interview with Alicia Munnell, October 18, 2017.

11. Merrill Lynch Wealth Management, "Home in Retirement: More Freedom, New Choices," retirement study conducted in partnership with Age Wave ([Charlotte, NC]: Bank of America Corporation, 2015), https://agewave.com/wp-content/uploads/2016/07/2015-ML-AW-Home-in-Retirement_More-Freedom-New-Choices.pdf. Also see Edleson, "Selling the Family Home."

12. "Part B Costs," Your Medicare Costs, Medicare.gov, accessed December 10, 2020, https://www.medicare.gov/your-medicare-costs/part-b-costs. Data also tallied from https://www.medicare.gov/plan-compare/#/?lang=en&year=2021 (log-in required). And see Centers for Medicare and Medicaid Services, *Medicare and You, 2021: The Official U.S. Government Medicare Handbook* (Baltimore: US Department of Health and Human Services, 2020), https://www.medicare.gov/sites/default/files/2020-09/10050-Medicare-and-You_0.pdf.

13. Or download the booklet in various formats at https://www.medicare.gov/forms-help-resources/medicare-you-handbook/download-medicare-you-in-different-formats.

14. "Part B Costs," Medicare.gov.

15. Edleson, "Taking a Job."

16. Ibid.

17. Ibid.

18. Ibid.

Chapter Three

1. Author phone interview with Bob McDonald, November 3, 2017.

2. Ibid.

3. Ibid.

4. Harriet Edleson, "For Older Couples, House-Hunting Begins with Soul-Searching," *New York Times*, August 15, 2014, https://www.nytimes.com/2014/08/16/your-money/for-older-couples-house-hunting-begins-with-soul-searching.html.

5. Ibid.

6. Ibid.

7. Ibid.

8. Ibid.

9. Author phone interview with Brian and Heather, January 2018.

10. Ibid.

11. Ibid.

12. George Kinder, *Life Planning for You: How to Design and Deliver the Life of Your Dreams*, with Mary Rowland ([Littleton, MA]: Serenity Point Press, 2014).

13. Author phone interview with George Kinder, August 2016.

14. Ibid.

15. Ibid.

16. Kinder, *Life Planning for You*, 57.

Chapter Four

1. Edleson, "How to Budget for Retirement."

2. Lynda Gratton and Andrew Scott, *The 100-Year Life: Living and Working in an Age of Longevity* (London: Bloomsbury Publishing, 2016); Edleson, "How to Budget for Retirement."

3. Edleson, "How to Budget for Retirement."

4. See the Social Security Administration's life-expectancy calculator at https://www.ssa.gov/oact/population/longevity.html.

5. Edleson, "How to Budget for Retirement."

6. Ibid.

7. Ibid.

8. Catherine Collinson, Patti Rowey, and Heidi Cho, *A Precarious Existence: How Today's Retirees Are Financially Faring in Retirement*, Transamerica Center for Retirement Studies report, December (Los Angeles: Transamerica Institute, 2018), https://www.transamericacenter.org/docs/default-source/retirees-survey/tcrs2018_sr_retirees_survey_financially_faring.pdf.

9. Check out Vanguard's worksheet at https://personal.vanguard.com/us/insights/retirement/tool/retirement-expense-worksheet.

10. Edleson, "How to Budget for Retirement."

11. Ibid.

Chapter Five

1. Parenthetical original, Collinson, *What Is "Retirement"?*

2. Ibid.

3. Author phone interview with John Tarnoff, January 9, 2018. And see John Tarnoff, *Baby Boomer Reinvention: How to Create Your Dream Career Over 50* (Los Angeles: Reinvention Press, 2017.

4. Author phone interview with Tarnoff.

5. Ibid.

6. Ibid.

7. Harriet Edleson, "After Years Out of a Job, Older Workers Find a Way Back In," *New York Times*, November 6, 2015, https://www.nytimes.com/2015/11/07/your-money/after-years-out-of-a-job-older-workers-find-a-way-back-in.html.

8. Ibid.

9. Ibid.

10. Ibid.

11. Social Security National Press Office, "Fact Sheet: Social Security," Social Security Administration, accessed December 10, 2020, https://www.ssa.gov/news/press/factsheets/colafacts2021.pdf.

12. Harriet Edleson, "Working after Retirement: Beware the Cost," AARP.org, September 12, 2018, https://www.aarp.org/retirement/planning-for-retirement/info-2018/going-back-to-work-ss.html.

13. Harriet Edleson, "Nearing Retirement? It's Time to Be Creative," *New York Times*, July 3, 2015, https://www.nytimes.com/2015/07/04/your-money/nearing-retirement-its-time-to-be-creative.html.

14. Edleson, "Retirement Savings Shortfall?"

15. Data via e-mail to author from public affairs personnel at the Social Security Administration, April, 2019.

16. Harriet Edleson, "How to Save for a Rainy Day and Emergencies," AARP.org, July 19, 2019, https://www.aarp.org/money/budgeting-saving/info-2019/rainy-day-emergency-fund.html.

17. Ibid.

18. Ibid.

19. Ibid.

20. John Ameriks, Joseph S. Briggs, Andrew Caplin, Minjoon Lee, Matthew D. Shapiro, and Christopher Tonetti, "Older Americans Would Work Longer if Jobs Were Flexible," working paper, National Bureau of Economic Research, November 2017, https://www.nber.org/papers/w24008.

21. Ibid., parentheticals original.

22. Office of Personnel Management, "OPM Issues Final Rule on Phased Retirement," news release, August 7, 2014, https://www.opm.gov/news/releases/2014/08opm-issues-final-rule-on-phased-retirement/.

23. Ibid.

24. Kerry Hannon, "How Working in Retirement Became a Reality," *Next Avenue*, September 6, 2019, https://www.nextavenue.org/working-in-retirement-reality/.

Chapter Six

1. "Update 2021," pub. no. 05-10003, Social Security Administration, January 2021, https://www.ssa.gov/pubs/EN-05-10003.pdf.

2. Harriet Edleson, "How to Maximize Your Social Security Benefit," *U.S. News & World Report*, January 8, 2014, https://money.usnews.com/money/personal-finance/articles/2014/01/08/how-to-maximize-your-social-security-benefit.

3. Calculated using the Social Security Administration's online retirement-age calculator, at https://www.ssa.gov/benefits/retirement/planner/ageincrease.html.

4. "A Summary of the 2020 Annual Reports," Social Security Administration, 2020, https://www.ssa.gov/oact/trsum/.

5. Harriet Edleson, "Keep an Eye on Your Social Security Earnings Record," AARP.org, October 5, 2018, https://www.aarp.org/retirement/social-security/info-2018/check-your-social-security-earnings.html.

6. Harriet Edleson, "Will Social Security Still Be There if I Wait to Claim It?" MarketWatch, January 29, 2021, https://www.marketwatch.com/story/will-social -security-still-be-there-if-i-wait-to-claim-it-2021-01-29.

7. "Mid-career," Social Security Administration, accessed December 9, 2020, https://www.ssa.gov/people/midcareer/.

8. Harriet Edleson, "Why Wait to Take Social Security? Optimal Timing Means You Earn More," AARP.org, July 26, 2019, https://www.aarp.org/retirement/social -security/info-2019/take-benefits-early-lose-money.html.

9. Doug Lemons, "When to Start Collecting Social Security Benefits: A Break-Even Analysis," *Journal of Financial Planning* 25, no. 1 (2012): 52–54, 56–60.

10. David M. Blanchett, "Optimal Social Security Claiming Strategies," *Journal of Personal Finance* 11, no. 2 (2012): 36–87.

11. Edleson, "How to Budget."

12. Ibid.

13. Calculated at https://www.ssa.gov/oact/population/longevity.html.

14. Society of Actuaries, "Deciding When to Claim Social Security."

15. Edleson, "How to Maximize Your Social Security Benefit." And see John D. Deppe, Angela S. Deppe, and Social Security Central LLC, *It's Your Money! Simple Strategies to Maximize Your Social Security Income* (Rolling Meadows, IL: Windy City Publishers, 2012).

16. Edleson, "How to Maximize Your Social Security Benefit."

17. Ibid.

18. Harriet Edleson, "When You Should Take Social Security," *U.S. News & World Report*, January 10, 2014, https://money.usnews.com/money/personal-finance /articles/2014/01/10/when-you-should-take-social-security.

19. Edleson, "How to Maximize Your Social Security Benefit."

20. Edleson, "When You Should Take Social Security." And see Mary Hunt, *The Smart Woman's Guide to Planning for Retirement: How to Save for Your Future Today* (Grand Rapids, MI: Revell, 2013).

21. Edleson, "When You Should Take Social Security."

22. "Retirement Benefits," Social Security Administration, accessed October 28, 2020, https://www.ssa.gov/benefits/retirement/.

23. Ibid.

24. Ibid.

25. Edleson, "How to Maximize Your Social Security Benefit."

26. SSA.gov.

27. SSA.gov.

28. SSA.gov.

29. SSA.gov.

Chapter Seven

1. Joanne Binette and Kerri Vasold, "2018 Home and Community Preferences: A National Survey of Adults Age 18-Plus," AARP, August 2018, revised July 2019, https://www.aarp.org/research/topics/community/info-2018/2018-home-community -preference.html.

2. Collinson, Rowey, and Cho, *A Precarious Existence*.

3. Harriet Edleson, "How to Massively Reduce Your Housing Costs Before Retirement," *U.S. News & World Report*, December 20, 2013, text available at https:// news.yahoo.com/massively-reduce-housing-costs-retirement-180250665.html. And see Jane Cullinane, *The Single Woman's Guide to Retirement* (Hoboken, NJ: John Wiley & Sons, Inc., 2012).

4. Edleson, "How to Massively Reduce Your Housing Costs."

5. Ibid.

6. Ibid.

7. Ibid.

8. Ibid.

9. Ibid.

10. Harriet Edleson, "Downsizing Offers a Fresh Start for Older Adults," *New York Times*, October 2, 2015, https://www.nytimes.com/2015/10/03/your-money /downsizing-offers-a-fresh-start-for-older-adults.html.

11. Ibid.

12. Harriet Edleson, "Now that the Nest Is Empty, Retirees Seek Housing Better Suited to Their Age and Households," *Washington Post*, November 23, 2016, https:// www.washingtonpost.com/realestate/the-nest-is-empty-now-what/2016/11/23 /0c5a5228-48fd-11e6-bdb9-701687974517_story.html.

13. Edleson, "Downsizing Offers a Fresh Start."

14. Edleson, "Now that the Nest Is Empty."

15. Ibid.

16. Ibid.

17. Edleson, "Selling the Family Home."

18. Harriet Edleson, "Grandparents Who Move to Be Closer to Grandchildren," *New York Times*, June 26, 2015, https://www.nytimes.com/2015/06/27/your-money /grandparents-who-move-to-be-closer-to-grandchildren.html.

19. Edleson, "How to Massively Reduce Your Housing Costs."

20. Ibid.

21. Harriet Edleson, "Looking for a Housemate, Not a Mate, in Later Life," *New York Times*, July 11, 2014, https://www.nytimes.com/2014/07/12/your-money /looking-for-a-housemate-not-a-mate-in-later-life.html.

22. Ibid.

23. Ibid.

24. Ibid. And for more information about shared living arrangements, visit https://www.womenlivingincommunity.com/.

25. Edleson, "Looking for a Housemate."

26. Visit the National Shared Housing Resource Center online at https://national sharedhousing.org/.

Chapter Eight

1. National Association of Personal Financial Advisors, "NAPFA Survey on the Financial Health of Americans—Generational Breakdown," January 2020, http://s3.napfa.cql-aws.com.s3.amazonaws.com/files/Pressroom/2020/NAPFA%20Full%20Survey%20Results%20Final.pdf.

2. Edleson, "Selling the Family Home."

3. Ibid.

4. Ibid.

5. Ibid.

6. Ibid.

7. Ibid.

8. Edleson, "Taking a Job."

9. Ibid.

10. Collinson, Rowey, and Cho, A Precarious Existence.

11. Harriet Edleson, "Selling Your Home to Fund Your Retirement Lifestyle: Do the Math to See if Extracting Cash Can Help You Live on Less," Next Avenue, March 2, 2015, https://www.nextavenue.org/selling-your-home-finance-your-retirement-lifestyle/.

12. Ibid.

13. Visit the National Association of Appraisers online at https://www.naappraisers.org/.

14. Visit the American Society of Appraisers online at https://www.appraisers.org/.

15. Audrey Ference, "What Is a Comparative Market Analysis? The CMA Explained," realtor.com, April 11, 2019, https://www.realtor.com/advice/sell/understanding-the-comparative-market-analysis/.

16. Michele Lerner, "What Do House Appraisals Cost? Must-Know Info for Buyers," realtor.com, February 18, 2014, https://www.realtor.com/advice/buy/what-you-should-know-about-the-appraisal-process/.

17. Harriet Edleson, "How to Save Money When You Move: Relocation Can Be Costly, So Be Sure to Plan Ahead," U.S. News & World Report, January 30, 2014, https://money.usnews.com/money/personal-finance/articles/2014/01/30/how-to-save-money-when-you-move.

18. National Association of Realtors, *2019 Home Buyer and Seller Generational Trends Report* (Washington, DC: National Association of Realtors, 2019), https://www.nar.realtor/sites/default/files/documents/2019-home-buyers-and-sellers-generational-trends-report-08-16-2019.pdf.

19. Ibid.

20. Edleson, "Taking a Job."

Chapter Nine

1. Harriet Edleson, "Retirement in a Community, but Which One," *New York Times*, March 6, 2015, https://www.nytimes.com/2015/03/07/your-money/retirement-in-a-community-but-which-one.html.

2. Ibid.

3. Ibid.

4. Ibid.

5. Ibid.

6. Ibid.

7. Ibid.

8. Ibid.

9. Anna Rappaport, *Are CCRCs and Senior Housing Communities a Good Choice? COVID-19 and Risk in Arrangements for Senior Housing and Support* (Schaumberg, IL: The Society of Actuaries, 2020).

10. Harriet Edleson, "How to Find the Right Active Adult Community," *Next Avenue*, June 10, 2015, https://www.nextavenue.org/how-to-find-the-right-active-adult-community/.

11. Edleson, "Retirement in a Community."

12. Ibid.

13. Ibid.

14. Harriet Edleson, "Advice on Moving to a Continuing Care Retirement Community," *Next Avenue*, February 23, 2016, https://www.nextavenue.org/advice-on-moving-to-a-continuing-care-retirement-community/.

15. Ibid.

16. Ibid.

17. Ibid.

18. CARF International, *Consumer Guide to Understanding Financial Performance and Reporting in Continuing Care Retirement Communities* (Tucson, AZ: CARF International, 2016), text retrieved from https://static1.squarespace.com/static/5898f6e4e6f2e17c07ec6bbf/t/5f2ac6ddc4fe64566150bb48/1596638946931/CCRC+Consumer+Guide+to+Financial+Performance+-+June+2016.pdf.

19. US Government Accountability Office, "Older Americans: Continuing Care Retirement Communities Can Provide Benefits, but Not without Some Risk," GAO-10-611, report to the chairman, Special Committee on Aging, US Senate, June 27, 2013, https://www.gao.gov/assets/310/305752.pdf.

20. Harriet Edleson, "How to Cope with Downsizing Your Home," AARP.org, August 8, 2019, https://www.aarp.org/retirement/planning-for-retirement/info-2019/coping-with-downsizing.html.

Chapter Ten

1. Collinson, Rowey, and Cho, *A Precarious Existence.*
2. Ibid.
3. Adrian D. Garcia, "These Are the Best and Worst States for Retirement," Bankrate.com, July 10, 2019, https://www.bankrate.com/retirement/best-and-worst-states-for-retirement/.
4. Author interview via phone with Rob, December 10, 2019.
5. Ibid.
6. Edleson, "Now that the Nest Is Empty."
7. Edleson, "Looking for a Housemate." And see Joan Medlicott, *The Ladies of Covington Send Their Love* (New York: St. Martins, 2000).
8. Ibid.
9. Office for Older Americans, Consumer Financial Protection Bureau, "Snapshot of Older Consumers."
10. Author telephone interview, April 2018.
11. Ibid.
12. Ibid.
13. H&R Block, "Which States Have No Income Tax?" Tax Information Center, H&R Block (website), accessed October 28, 2020, https://www.hrblock.com/tax-center/filing/states/states-with-no-income-tax/.
14. Ibid.
15. Ibid.
16. Social Security Administration, "Understanding the Benefits," pub. no. 05-10024, SSA.gov, January 2021, https://www.ssa.gov/pubs/EN-05-10024.pdf.
17. Internal Revenue Service, *Tax Guide for Seniors, for Use in Preparing 2019 Returns,* IRS publication no. 554, December 27 (Washington, DC: US Department of the Treasury, 2019), https://www.irs.gov/pub/irs-pdf/p554.pdf. And also see "Forms Related to Publication 554," IRS.gov, last reviewed or updated September 25, 2020, https://www.irs.gov/forms-pubs/about-publication-554-related-forms.

Chapter Eleven

1. Harriet Edleson, "When Planning for Retirement, Consider Transportation," *New York Times,* October 17, 2014, https://www.nytimes.com/2014/10/18/your-money/when-retirement-planning-consider-transportation.html.
2. Ibid.

3. Daniel J. Foley, Harley K. Heimovitz, Jack M. Guralnik, and Dwight B. Brock, "Driving Life Expectancy of Persons Aged 70 and Older in the United States," *American Journal of Public Health* 92, no. 8 (2002): 1284–89, https://ajph.aphapublications.org/doi/epub/10.2105/AJPH.92.8.1284.

4. Katherine Freund, Alycia Bayne, Alexa Siegfried, Joe Warren, Tori Nadel, Amarjothi Natarajan, and Laurie Beck, "Environmental Scan of Ride Share Services Available for Older Adults," white paper, National Opinion Research Center at the University of Chicago and ITNAmerica, December 5, 2019, https://reports.norc.org/white_paper/environmental-scan-of-ride-share-services-available-for-older-adults/.

5. Ibid. And see Edleson, "When Planning for Retirement."

6. Vanya C. Jones, Renee M. Johnson, Carey Borkoski, Andrea C. Gielen, and George W. Rebok, "Perceived Social Support Differences between Male and Female Older Adults Who Have Reduced Driving: AAA LongRoad Study," research brief, AAA Foundation for Traffic Safety, February 2020, https://aaafoundation.org/wp-content/uploads/2020/02/20-0009_AAAFTS_LongROAD-Social-Support-Brief_r1-1.pdf. And see Freund et al., "Environmental Scan of Ride Share Services."

7. Freund et al., ""Environmental Scan of Ride Share Services."

8. Edleson, "When Planning for Retirement."

9. Author telephone interview with John Lemega, January 27, 2020.

10. Ibid.

11. Ibid.

12. Ibid.

13. Edleson, "When Planning for Retirement."

14. Judi Bonilla, *Freewheeling after Sixty: Design Your Personalized Transportation System* (Carlsbad, CA: Advocates For Aging, 2016).

15. Harriet Edleson, "Going Places without a Car in Retirement," Kiplinger, June 29, 2020, https://www.kiplinger.com/retirement/600971/going-places-without-a-car-in-retirement.

16. Author telephone interview with Maria, March, 10, 2020.

17. Ibid.

18. Harriet Edleson, "How to Plan for When You Can No Longer Drive: Tips to Make Transportation Easier Once You Need Help Getting Around," *Next Avenue*, April 19, 2016, https://www.nextavenue.org/how-to-plan-for-when-you-can-no-longer-drive/.

19. Edleson, "When Planning for Retirement."

20. Harriet Edleson, "When Planning for Retirement."

21. Edleson, "How to Plan for When You Can No Longer Drive."

22. Ibid.

23. Ibid.

Chapter Twelve

1. This prediction, of course, represents an important trend, even if the global COVID-19 pandemic has depressed these numbers. See Vicki Levy, "Boomers Have Big Travel Plans in 2020," 2020 Travel Trends, AARP Research, Issues and Topics, Life and Leisure, AARP.org, January 2020, https://www.aarp.org/research/topics/life/info-2019/2020-travel-trends.html.

2. Ibid.

3. Barbara Peterson, "Where Can I Travel and Do I Need the COVID-19 Vaccine?" *Wall Street Journal*, February 4, 2021, https://www.wsj.com/articles/where-can-i-travel-internationally-and-do-i-need-the-covid-19-vaccine-11612469432.

4. Harriet Edleson, "Offbeat Ways to Make Travel Affordable," *New York Times*, August 14, 2015, https://www.nytimes.com/2015/08/15/your-money/offbeat-ways-to-make-travel-affordable.html.

5. Harriet Edleson, "There's Still Time to Score an Affordable Summer Getaway: Flexibility Is Key to Getting a Good Deal," AARP.org, July 17, 2019, https://www.aarp.org/travel/travel-tips/budget/info-2019/affordable-summer-getaways.html.

6. Edleson, "Offbeat Ways to Make Travel Affordable."

7. Ibid.

8. Ibid.

9. Ibid.

10. Ibid.

11. Ibid.

12. Ibid.

13. Ibid.

14. Edleson, "There's Still Time."

15. Ibid.

16. Ibid.

17. Edleson, "Offbeat Ways to Make Travel Affordable."

18. Glenn Ruffenach, "Podcast: Tips for Doing a Home Exchange: Agreeing to Swap Homes for Vacation Saves Money, but Adds Complications," *Wall Street Journal*, March 21, 2017, https://www.wsj.com/articles/podcast-tips-for-doing-a-home-exchange-1490128841.

19. Ibid.

20. Harriet Edleson, "How to Get a Good Deal on a Midwinter Vacation," *U.S. News & World Report*, December 30, 2013, text retrieved from https://news.yahoo.com/good-deal-midwinter-vacation-165113210.html. See also https://www.medicare.gov/coverage/travel.

21. Edleson, "Offbeat Ways to Make Travel Affordable."

22. Ibid.

23. Lisa Lake, "Make It a Scam-Free Vacation," Consumer Information, Federal Trade Commission, May 23, 2019, https://www.consumer.ftc.gov/blog/2019/05/make-it-scam-free-vacation.

24. Harriet Edleson, "Auto, Home and Retail Top Consumer Complaint List: Local and State Agencies Work to Resolve Individual Problems," AARP.org, September 11, 2019, https://www.aarp.org/money/scams-fraud/info-2019/top-consumer-complaints.html.

25. Marc E. Agronin, "It's Time to Rethink the Bucket-List Retirement," *Wall Street Journal*, updated March 20, 2016, https://www.wsj.com/articles/its-time-to-rethink-the-bucket-list-retirement-1458525877.

26. Ibid.

27. Ibid.

Bibliography

Agronin, Marc E. "It's Time to Rethink the Bucket-List Retirement." *Wall Street Journal*, updated March 20, 2016. https://www.wsj.com/articles/its-time-to-rethink -the-bucket-list-retirement-1458525877.

Ameriks, John, Joseph S. Briggs, Andrew Caplin, Minjoon Lee, Matthew D. Shapiro, and Christopher Tonetti. "Older Americans Would Work Longer if Jobs Were Flexible." Working paper. National Bureau of Economic Research, November 2017. https://www.nber.org/papers/w24008.

ATTOM staff. "Q3 2019 Foreclosure Activity Down 19 Percent from Year Ago to Lowest Level since Q2 2005." Attom Data Solutions, October 15, 2019. https:// www.attomdata.com/news/market-trends/attom-data-solutions-q3-2019-u-s-fore closure-market-report/.

Binette, Joanne, and Kerri Vasold. "2018 Home and Community Preferences: A National Survey of Adults Age 18-Plus." AARP, August 2018, revised July 2019. https://www.aarp.org/research/topics/community/info-2018/2018-home-commu nity-preference.html.

Blanchett, David M. "Optimal Social Security Claiming Strategies." *Journal of Personal Finance* 11, no. 2 (2012): 36–87.

Board of Governors of the Federal Reserve System. *Survey of Consumer Finances, 1989–2019.* Federal Reserve System, last updated September 28, 2020. https://www .federalreserve.gov/econres/scf/dataviz/scf/chart/#series:Retirement_Accounts ;demographic:agecl;population:all;units:median.

Bonilla, Judi. *Freewheeling after Sixty: Design Your Personalized Transportation System.* Carlsbad, CA: Advocates for Aging, 2016.

CARF International. *Consumer Guide to Understanding Financial Performance and Reporting in Continuing Care Retirement Communities.* Tucson, AZ: CARF

International, 2016. Text retrieved from https://static1.squarespace.com /static/5898f6e4e6f2e17c07ec6bbf/t/5f2ac6ddc4fe64566150bb48/1596638946931 /CCRC+Consumer+Guide+to+Financial+Performance+-+June+2016.pdf.

Center for Retirement Research at Boston College. "Frequently Requested Data: Workers with Pension Coverage by Type of Plan, 1983, 1998, and 2016." Last updated February 2018. http://crr.bc.edu/wp-content/uploads/2015/10/figure-16.pdf.

Centers for Medicare and Medicaid Services. *Medicare and You, 2021: The Official U.S. Government Medicare Handbook.* Baltimore: US Department of Health and Human Services, 2020. https://www.medicare.gov/sites/default/files /2020-09/10050-Medicare-and-You_0.pdf.

Collinson, Catherine. *Retirement through the Ages: Expectations and Preparations of American Workers.* Transamerica Center for Retirement Studies report, May. Los Angeles: Transamerica Institute, 2015. https://www.transamericacenter .org/docs/default-source/resources/center-research/16th-annual/tcrs2015_sr_retire ment_throughout_the_ages.pdf.

Collinson, Catherine, Patti [Vogt] Rowey, and Heidi Cho. *A Precarious Existence: How Today's Retirees Are Financially Faring in Retirement.* Transamerica Center for Retirement Studies report, December. Los Angeles: Transamerica Institute, 2018. https://www.transamericacenter.org/docs/default-source/retirees-survey/tcrs2018 _sr_retirees_survey_financially_faring.pdf.

———. *Retirement Security: A Compendium of Findings about US Workers; 20th Annual Transamerica Retirement Survey of Workers.* Transamerica Center for Retirement Studies, December 2020. https://transamericacenter.org/docs/default-source /retirement-survey-of-workers/tcrs2020_sr_20th_annual_compendium_of_work ers_report.pdf.

———. *What Is "Retirement"? Three Generations Prepare for Older Age: 19th Annual Transamerica Retirement Survey of Workers.* Transamerica Center for Retirement Studies report, April. Los Angeles: Transamerica Institute, 2019. https://trans americacenter.org/docs/default-source/retirement-survey-of-workers/tcrs2019_sr _what_is_retirement_by_generation.pdf.

Consumer Financial Protection Bureau. "CFPB Spotlights Mortgage Debt Challenges Faced by Older Americans." Newsroom, May 7, 2014. https://www.consumer finance.gov/about-us/newsroom/cfpb-spotlights-mortgage-debt-challenges-faced -by-older-americans/.

Cullinane, Jan. *The Single Woman's Guide to Retirement.* Hoboken, NJ: John Wiley & Sons, Inc., 2012.

Deppe, John D., Angela S. Deppe, and Social Security Central LLC. *It's Your Money! Simple Strategies to Maximize Your Social Security Income.* Rolling Meadows, IL: Windy City Publishers, 2012.

Edleson, Harriet. "Advice on Moving to a Continuing Care Retirement Community." *Next Avenue,* February 23, 2016. https://www.nextavenue.org/advice-on -moving-to-a-continuing-care-retirement-community/.

———. "After Years Out of a Job, Older Workers Find a Way Back In." *New York Times*, November 6, 2015. https://www.nytimes.com/2015/11/07/your-money /after-years-out-of-a-job-older-workers-find-a-way-back-in.html.

———. "Almost Half of Americans Fear Running Out of Money in Retirement." AARP.org, May 21, 2019. https://www.aarp.org/retirement/planning-for-retire ment/info-2019/retirees-fear-losing-money.html.

———. "Auto, Home and Retail Top Consumer Complaint List: Local and State Agencies Work to Resolve Individual Problems." AARP.org, September 11, 2019. https://www.aarp.org/money/scams-fraud/info-2019/top-consumer-complaints .html.

———. "Downsizing Offers a Fresh Start for Older Adults." *New York Times*, October 2, 2015. https://www.nytimes.com/2015/10/03/your-money/downsizing-offers -a-fresh-start-for-older-adults.html.

———. "For Older Couples, House-Hunting Begins with Soul-Searching." *New York Times*, August 15, 2014. https://www.nytimes.com/2014/08/16/your-money /for-older-couples-house-hunting-begins-with-soul-searching.html.

———. "Going Places without a Car in Retirement." Kiplinger, June 29, 2020. https://www.kiplinger.com/retirement/600971/going-places-without-a-car-in -retirement.

———. "Grandparents Who Move to Be Closer to Grandchildren." *New York Times*, June 26, 2015. https://www.nytimes.com/2015/06/27/your-money/grandparents -who-move-to-be-closer-to-grandchildren.html.

———. "How to Budget for Retirement: Running the Numbers Is Key if You're within Five Years of Retirement." *Next Avenue*, August 16, 2016. https://www .nextavenue.org/how-to-budget-for-retirement/.

———. "How to Cope with Downsizing Your Home." AARP.org, August 8, 2019. https://www.aarp.org/retirement/planning-for-retirement/info-2019/coping-with -downsizing.html.

———. "How to Find the Right Active Adult Community." *Next Avenue*, June 10, 2015. https://www.nextavenue.org/how-to-find-the-right-active-adult-community/.

———. "How to Get a Good Deal on a Midwinter Vacation," *U.S. News & World Report*, December 30, 2013. Text retrieved from https://news.yahoo.com/good -deal-midwinter-vacation-165113210.html,

———. "How to Massively Reduce Your Housing Costs Before Retirement." *U.S. News & World Report*, December 20, 2013. Text available at https://news.yahoo .com/massively-reduce-housing-costs-retirement-180250665.html.

———. "How to Maximize Your Social Security Benefit." *U.S. News & World Report*, January 8, 2014. https://money.usnews.com/money/personal-finance/articles /2014/01/08/how-to-maximize-your-social-security-benefit.

———. "How to Plan for When You Can No Longer Drive: Tips to Make Transportation Easier Once You Need Help Getting Around." *Next Avenue*, April 19, 2016. https://www.nextavenue.org/how-to-plan-for-when-you-can-no-longer-drive/.

———. "How to Save for a Rainy Day and Emergencies." AARP.org, July 19, 2019. https://www.aarp.org/money/budgeting-saving/info-2019/rainy-day-emergency-fund.html.

———. "How to Save Money When You Move: Relocation Can Be Costly, So Be Sure to Plan Ahead." *U.S. News & World Report*, January 30, 2014. https://money.usnews.com/money/personal-finance/articles/2014/01/30/how-to-save-money-when-you-move

———. "Keep an Eye on Your Social Security Earnings Record." AARP.org, October 5, 2018. https://www.aarp.org/retirement/social-security/info-2018/check-your-social-security-earnings.html.

———. "Looking for a Housemate, Not a Mate, in Later Life." *New York Times*, July 11, 2014. https://www.nytimes.com/2014/07/12/your-money/looking-for-a-housemate-not-a-mate-in-later-life.html.

———. "Nearing Retirement? It's Time to Be Creative." *New York Times*, July 3, 2015. https://www.nytimes.com/2015/07/04/your-money/nearing-retirement-its-time-to-be-creative.html.

———. "Now that the Nest Is Empty, Retirees Seek Housing Better Suited to Their Age and Households." *Washington Post*, November 23, 2016. https://www.washingtonpost.com/realestate/the-nest-is-empty-now-what/2016/11/23/0c5a5228-48fd-11e6-bdb9-701687974517_story.html.

———. "Offbeat Ways to Make Travel Affordable." *New York Times*, August 14, 2015. https://www.nytimes.com/2015/08/15/your-money/offbeat-ways-to-make-travel-affordable.html.

———. "Retirement in a Community, but Which One," *New York Times*, March 6, 2015. https://www.nytimes.com/2015/03/07/your-money/retirement-in-a-community-but-which-one.html.

———. "Retirement Savings Shortfall? Get a Part-Time Job: Finding the Right Type of Work Might Require Some Type of Creativity." *Next Avenue*, August 18, 2015. https://www.nextavenue.org/retirement-savings-shortfall-get-a-part-time-job/.

———. "Selling the Family Home Is Liberating for Many Retirees." *New York Times*, October 19, 2014. https://www.nytimes.com/2014/12/20/your-money/selling-the-family-home-is-liberating-for-many-retirees.html.

———. "Selling Your Home to Fund Your Retirement Lifestyle: Do the Math to See if Extracting Cash Can Help You Live on Less." *Next Avenue*, March 2, 2015. https://www.nextavenue.org/selling-your-home-finance-your-retirement-lifestyle/.

———. "Taking a Job Out of the Financial Equation." *New York Times*, April 18, 2014. https://www.nytimes.com/2014/04/19/your-money/taking-a-job-out-of-the-financial-equation.html.

———. "There's Still Time to Score an Affordable Summer Getaway: Flexibility Is Key to Getting a Good Deal." AARP.org, July 17, 2019. https://www.aarp.org/travel/travel-tips/budget/info-2019/affordable-summer-getaways.html.

———. "When Planning for Retirement, Consider Transportation." *New York Times*, October 17, 2014. https://www.nytimes.com/2014/10/18/your-money /when-retirement-planning-consider-transportation.html.

———. "When You Should Take Social Security." *U.S. News & World Report*, January 10, 2014. https://money.usnews.com/money/personal-finance/articles /2014/01/10/when-you-should-take-social-security.

———. "Why Wait to Take Social Security? Optimal Timing Means You Earn More." AARP.org, July 26, 2019. https://www.aarp.org/retirement/social-security /info-2019/take-benefits-early-lose-money.html.

———. "Will Social Security Still Be There if I Wait to Claim It?" MarketWatch, January 29, 2021, https://www.marketwatch.com/story/will-social-security-still-be -there-if-i-wait-to-claim-it-2021-01-29.

———. "Working after Retirement: Beware the Cost." AARP.org, September 12, 2018. https://www.aarp.org/retirement/planning-for-retirement/info-2018/going -back-to-work-ss.html.

Ference, Audrey. "What Is a Comparative Market Analysis? The CMA Explained." realtor.com, April 11, 2019. https://www.realtor.com/advice/sell/understanding -the-comparative-market-analysis/.

Foley, Daniel J., Harley K. Heimovitz, Jack M. Guralnik, and Dwight B. Brock. "Driving Life Expectancy of Persons Aged 70 and Older in the United States." *American Journal of Public Health* 92, no. 8 (2002): 1284–89. https://ajph.aphapub lications.org/doi/epub/10.2105/AJPH.92.8.1284.

Freund, Katherine, Alycia Bayne, Alexa Siegfried, Joe Warren, Tori Nadel, Amarjothi Natarajan, and Laurie Beck. "Environmental Scan of Ride Share Services Available for Older Adults." White paper. National Opinion Research Center at the University of Chicago and ITNAmerica, December 5, 2019. https://reports .norc.org/white_paper/environmental-scan-of-ride-share-services-available-for -older-adults/.

Fry, Richard. "Americans Are Moving at Historically Low Rates, in Part Because Millennials Are Staying Put." Fact Tank, Pew Research Center, February 13, 2017. https://www.pewresearch.org/fact-tank/2017/02/13/americans-are-moving -at-historically-low-rates-in-part-because-millennials-are-staying-put/.

———. "The Pace of Boomer Retirements Has Accelerated in the Past Year." Fact Tank, Pew Research Center, November 9, 2020. https://www.pewresearch.org /fact-tank/2020/11/09/the-pace-of-boomer-retirements-has-accelerated-in-the -past-year/.

Garcia, Adrian D. "These Are the Best and Worst States for Retirement." Bankrate. com, July 10, 2019. https://www.bankrate.com/retirement/best-and-worst-states -for-retirement/.

Gratton, Lynda, and Andrew Scott. *The 100-Year Life: Living and Working in an Age of Longevity*. London: Bloomsbury Publishing, 2016.

H&R Block. "Which States Have No Income Tax?" Tax Information Center. H&R Block (website). Accessed October 28, 2020. https://www.hrblock.com/tax-center /filing/states/states-with-no-income-tax/.

Hannon, Kerry. "How Working in Retirement Became a Reality." *Next Avenue*, September 6, 2019. https://www.nextavenue.org/working-in-retirement-reality/.

Hinkle, Mark. "Social Security Announces 1.3 Percent Benefit Increase for 2021." Press release, Social Security Administration, October 13, 2020. https://www.ssa .gov/news/press/releases/2020/#10-2020-1.

Hunt, Mary. *The Smart Woman's Guide to Planning for Retirement: How to Save for Your Future Today.* Grand Rapids, MI: Revell, 2013.

Hurd, Michael D., and Susann Rohwedder. "Economic Preparation for Retirement." NBER working paper #17203, July 8. Cambridge, MA: National Bureau of Economic Research, 2011. https://www.nber.org/system/files/working_papers/w17203 /w17203.pdf.

Internal Revenue Service. *Tax Guide for Seniors, for Use in Preparing 2019 Returns.* IRS publication no. 554, December 27. Washington, DC: US Department of the Treasury, 2019. https://www.irs.gov/pub/irs-pdf/p554.pdf.

———. "Forms Related to Publication 554." IRS.gov, last reviewed or updated September 25, 2020. https://www.irs.gov/forms-pubs/about-publication-554-related -forms.

Jones, Vanya C., Renee M. Johnson, Carey Borkoski, Andrea C. Gielen, and George W. Rebok. "Perceived Social Support Differences between Male and Female Older Adults Who Have Reduced Driving: AAA LongRoad Study." Research brief, AAA Foundation for Traffic Safety, February 2020. https://aaafoundation.org /wp-content/uploads/2020/02/20-0009_AAAFTS_LongROAD-Social-Support -Brief_r1-1.pdf.

Kinder, George. *Life Planning for You: How to Design and Deliver the Life of Your Dreams.* With Mary Rowland. [Littleton, MA]: Serenity Point Press, 2014.

Lake, Lisa. "Make It a Scam-Free Vacation." Consumer Information, Federal Trade Commission, May 23, 2019. https://www.consumer.ftc.gov/blog/2019/05/make-it -scam-free-vacation.

Lemons, Doug. "When to Start Collecting Social Security Benefits: A Break-Even Analysis." *Journal of Financial Planning* 25, no. 1 (2012): 52–54, 56–60.

Lerner, Michele, "What Do House Appraisals Cost? Must-Know Info for Buyers." realtor.com, February 18, 2014. https://www.realtor.com/advice/buy/what-you -should-know-about-the-appraisal-process/.

Levy, Vicki. "Boomers Have Big Travel Plans in 2020." 2020 Travel Trends, AARP Research, Issues and Topics, Life and Leisure. AARP.org, January 2020. https:// www.aarp.org/research/topics/life/info-2019/2020-travel-trends.html.

Medicare.gov. "Part B Costs." Your Medicare Costs. Accessed December 10, 2020. https://www.medicare.gov/your-medicare-costs/part-b-costs.

Medlicott, Joan. *The Ladies of Covington Send Their Love.* New York: St. Martins, 2000.

Merrill Lynch Wealth Management. "Home in Retirement: More Freedom, New Choices." Retirement study conducted in partnership with Age Wave. [Charlotte, NC]: Bank of America Corporation, 2015. https://agewave.com/wp-content/uploads/2016/07/2015-ML-AW-Home-in-Retirement_More-Freedom-New-Choices.pdf.

National Association of Personal Financial Advisors. "NAPFA Survey on the Financial Health of Americans—Generational Breakdown." January 2020. http://s3.napfa.cql-aws.com.s3.amazonaws.com/files/Pressroom/2020/NAPFA%20Full%20Survey%20Results%20Final.pdf.

National Association of Realtors. *2019 Home Buyer and Seller Generational Trends Report*. Washington, DC: National Association of Realtors, 2019. https://www.nar.realtor/sites/default/files/documents/2019-home-buyers-and-sellers-generational-trends-report-08-16-2019.pdf.

Office for Older Americans, Consumer Financial Protection Bureau. "Snapshot of Older Consumers and Mortgage Debt." May 2014. https://files.consumerfinance.gov/f/201405_cfpb_snapshot_older-consumers-mortgage-debt.pdf.

Office of Personnel Management. "OPM Issues Final Rule on Phased Retirement." News release, August 7, 2014. https://www.opm.gov/news/releases/2014/08/opm-issues-final-rule-on-phased-retirement/.

Peterson, Barbara. "Where Can I Travel and Do I Need the COVID-19 Vaccine?" *Wall Street Journal*, February 4, 2021, https://www.wsj.com/articles/where-can-i-travel-internationally-and-do-i-need-the-covid-19-vaccine-11612469432.

Rappaport, Anna. *Are CCRCs and Senior Housing Communities a Good Choice? COVID-19 and Risk in Arrangements for Senior Housing and Support*. Schaumberg, IL: The Society of Actuaries, 2020.

Ruffenach, Glenn. "Podcast: Tips for Doing a Home Exchange: Agreeing to Swap Homes for Vacation Saves Money, but Adds Complications." *Wall Street Journal*, March 21, 2017. https://www.wsj.com/articles/podcast-tips-for-doing-a-home-exchange-1490128841.

Saad, Lydia. "What Percentage of Americans Owns Stock?" The Short Answer. Gallup, September 13, 2019. https://news.gallup.com/poll/266807/percentage-americans-owns-stock.aspx.

Social Security Administration. "Mid-career." SSA.gov, accessed December 9, 2020. https://www.ssa.gov/people/midcareer/.

———. "Retirement and Survivor's Benefits: Life Expectancy Calculator." SSA.gov, accessed December 16, 2020. https://www.ssa.gov/OACT/population/longevity.html.

———. "Retirement Benefits." SSA.gov, accessed October 28, 2020. https://www.ssa.gov/benefits/retirement/.

———. "A Summary of the 2020 Annual Reports: Social Security and Medicare Boards of Trustees." SSA.gov, accessed October 28, 2020. https://www.ssa.gov/OACT/TRSUM/index.html.

———. "Update 2021." Publication no. 05-10003, SSA.gov, January 2021. https://www.ssa.gov/pubs/EN-05-10003.pdf.

———. "Understanding the Benefits." Publication no. 05-10024, Social Security Administration, January 2021. https://www.ssa.gov/pubs/EN-05-10024.pdf.

———. "When to Start Receiving Retirement Benefits." Publication no. 05-10147, SSA.gov, January 2021. https://www.ssa.gov/pubs/EN-05-10147.pdf.

Social Security National Press Office. "Fact Sheet: Social Security." Social Security Administration, accessed December 10, 2020. https://www.ssa.gov/news/press/factsheets/colafacts2021.pdf.

Society of Actuaries. "Deciding When to Claim Social Security." Managing Retirement Decisions Series, 2017. https://www.soa.org/globalassets/assets/Files/Research/research-pen-deciding-ss.pdf.

Society of Actuaries Committee on Post Retirement Needs and Risks, Urban Institute, and Women's Institute for a Secure Retirement. "The Impact of Running Out of Money in Retirement." November 2012. https://www.wiserwomen.org/wp-content/uploads/2018/01/Impact-running-out-of-money-retirement-report-2012.pdf.

Tarnoff, John. Baby Boomer Reinvention: How to Create Your Dream Career Over 50. Los Angeles: Reinvention Press, 2017.

Transamerica Center for Retirement. "The Pandemic's Impact on Workers' Finances Has Long-Term Repercussions for Retirement Security." Press release, December 18, 2020. https://transamericacenter.org/docs/default-source/retirement-survey-of-workers/tcrs2020_pr_20th_annual_worker_compendium_press_release.pdf.

US Government Accountability Office. "Older Americans: Continuing Care Retirement Communities Can Provide Benefits, but Not without Some Risk." GAO-10-611, report to the chairman, Special Committee on Aging, US Senate, June 27, 2013. https://www.gao.gov/assets/310/305752.pdf.

Vanguard Group. "Retirement Expenses Worksheet." Accessed October 28, 2020. https://personal.vanguard.com/us/insights/retirement/tool/retirement-expense-worksheet.

———. "Retirement Income Worksheet." Accessed October 28, 2020. https://personal.vanguard.com/us/insights/retirement/tool/retirement-income-worksheet.

Index

~

About the Author

Harriet Edleson is an expert on baby boomer retirement strategies. A former staff writer for AARP and contributing writer for *Kiplinger's Retirement Report*, she has written the Retiring feature for the *New York Times*. A graduate of Mount Holyoke College, she began her journalism career at Gannett Westchester (New York) newspapers and the *Houston Chronicle*. She writes for MarketWatch.com and the *Washington Post* Real Estate section, and lives in Bethesda, Maryland. Visit her website at https:// www.howtoretireonless.com.